What's
Possible!

Praise for *What's Possible!*

"A Sufi mystic once said, "When the heart weeps for what it's lost, the soul rejoices for what it's found." Daryn Kagan's beautiful book tells us stories of ordinary people who have endured extraordinary losses. And page after page we read about souls who have rejoiced for what they found. Each one has found something different yet spectacular: renewed faith in themselves, the ability to love others, the discovery that one can be broken and still be whole. When I finished this book, I felt better. Better about the world and better about what is possible. I think every newspaper editor and every TV news producer should be required to read this book and then reconsider what is truly newsworthy." —Dr. Dan Gottlieb, author of *Letters to Sam: A Grandfather's Lessons on Love, Loss, and the Gifts of Life*

"*What's Possible!* takes you on an inspiring journey that opens the door to the fulfillment of your dreams. After reading these amazing stories of courage, passion, and creativity, you can't help but believe that you have the power to make a difference in your life too!" —Cheryl Richardson, author of *The Unmistakable Touch of Grace: How to Recognize and Respond to the Spiritual Signposts in Your Life*

"Truly inspiring! Every few pages opens the world to another brave, awesome, yet—and this is the best part—*real* person reaching for the life he or she was destined to live. I'm ready to go run my marathon." —Jean Chatzky, author of *Make Money, Not Excuses*

What's
Possible!

50 True Stories of People
Who Dared to Dream
They Could Make a Difference

by
Daryn Kagan

Meredith® Books
Des Moines, IA

Meredith Books
1716 Locust Street
Des Moines, Iowa 50309–3023
meredithbooks.com

Cover photo by Marvin Scott

Printed in the United States of America.

First Edition.

Library of Congress Control Number: 2007938177
ISBN: 978-0-696-23891-8

Dedication

· ·

To my teachers and guides. Thank you for waiting for my open heart and pointing me toward the life I'm meant to live.

Table of Contents

What's Possible! Daryn Kagan 10

Defying the Odds:
Overcoming Physical
Challenges

No Excuses 28
Double amputee Scott Rigsby makes history at the Iron Man Triathlon in Hawaii.

It's Not About the Sculptures 34
Bill Montgomery learns to sculpt at age 80 after losing his sight.

Healing Myself,
Healing the World 38
Losing weight is a losing battle until George Roundy finds his motivation in raising money to help the hungry.

Born with a Mark of Greatness 42
Teen musician Stephen Dale sees facial difference as his source of strength.

Raisin Hope 46
Professional cyclist Saul Raisin keeps getting back on his bike no matter what life throws his way—including brain injury, curvature of the spine, and doctors who insist he give up his dream of riding in the Tour de France.

Survivor Stories:
Claiming Health and Healing

Feel Your Boobies® 53
Breast cancer survivor Leigh Hurst launches an upbeat campaign to encourage women to know their bodies and protect their health.

Beauty from the Bad 58
Makeup artist Ramy Gafni beats lymphoma and unemployment as he creates his own line of beauty products and helps other cancer patients.

Dead and Alive 63
Surviving cancer and heart surgery, Megan Kelley Hall focuses on developing her gift of writing.

One Step at a Time 68
Heart transplant recipient Kelly Perkins climbs mountains, promotes organ donation, and inspires others.

Champion Teammates 73
Sportswriter Steve Rom survives leukemia with the help of his friend, Super Bowl champion Rod Payne.

The Bald Truth 78
Soap opera actress Amy Gibson embraces her own hair loss and helps other women find beauty despite baldness.

An Orchard Full
of Good People 83
Mary Anne Tillman's search for a hit-and-run driver leads her to grant forgiveness.

Dreaming Big:
In Pursuit of a Passion

A 21-Year Lesson Plan 88
Along with building a family of adopted and biological children, Sharon Hayes-Brown patiently pursues a college degree.

Lifting the Heaviest
of Dreams 93
Age is no obstacle for champion weightlifter Melanie Roach.

My Head in the Clouds 97
It's a bird! It's a plane! No, it's Kent Couch and his flying lawn chair!

Painting Myself
Out of a Corner 101
Artist Dan Dunn reinvents his career with a little help from YouTube.

Composing My Dream Orchestra 106
Twentysomething conductor Alondra de la Parra shines the light on classical music from her beloved Latin America.

Finding Your Magic 110
NFL player Jon Dorenbos works magic on and off the field.

Yosemite Facelift 114
Rock climber Ken Yager organizes thousands of people annually to clean up this beautiful national park.

Giving Back:
Ordinary People,
Extraordinary Humanitarians

A Hospital for Harar 119
Building a hospital in his hometown of Harar, Ethiopian immigrant Sebri Omer shows that living the American dream can mean *not* waiting until you're wealthy to make a huge impact on the lives of others.

Fulfilling Children's Dreams 123
Holocaust survivor Henri Landwirth devotes his energy and resources to creating happy experiences for sick children.

Cartridges for a Cure® 128
Teenage leukemia survivor Eli Kahn devises a creative way to raise money for cancer research and to help the environment.

The Million-Dollar Resale Shop 132
Marie Hesser tells how a group of determined women in Stillwater, Oklahoma, overcomes lack of experience and know-how to establish a consignment shop that's helping their town.

Changing Gang Mentality 136
Former gang member Ernesto Luis Romero dedicates himself to helping kids choose a different life.

Compassion in Action 140
Appalled at the suffering of women in Bosnian rape camps, Zainab Salbi helps women war refugees around the world.

Frozen Inspiration 145
An abundance of breast milk stored in her freezer leads new mother Jill Youse to create the International Breast Milk Project.

Saving the Children 150
Abandoned on the streets of Soweto, South Africa, Bob Nameng survived thanks to one woman's kindness. Now he's working to rescue other orphans.

Desperate Escape 154
Trapped in an abusive marriage in a foreign country, Paula Lucas managed to save herself and her sons and now seeks to help others like her.

Bringing Babies to My House 159
What difference can one person make tackling a complex social problem? Plenty. Atlanta social worker Donna Carson shows how.

Serving Up Inspiration 164
Garth Larsen was frustrated with a lack of professional opportunities for his physically disabled son, Max. So together they create what they sought, a restaurant that offers job training, hope, confidence, and good food.

Creating Opportunity One Bite at a Time 169
Investment banker Alicia Polak walks away from a six-figure job to create a business and bakery in South Africa.

The Castaway Daughter 173
Marilyn Tam, one-time president of Reebok's apparel and retail group, tells how her experience as a child laborer in China shaped her mission in life.

Proved Innocent 178
After 10 years in prison for a crime he didn't commit, Ken Wyniemko reclaims his life.

Working Through Grief:
Healing Acts

Art with a Heart 184
Working with sick children allows artist
Lori Guadagno to pay tribute to her brother,
who died on 9/11.

Ben's Bells 190
Jeannette Maré-Packard finds distributing
symbols of kindness helps her family heal
after the sudden death of her young son.

Writer of Merit 194
Novelist Jacquelyn Mitchard works through her
grief to produce her first best seller and fulfill
her dying husband's prediction of success.

Prescription 4 Love 198
In honor of his late brother, Ricky Durham
develops a matchmaking website for people
living with chronic illnesses.

Shoulders to the Sky 202
Greg Rice faces the challenge of redefining his
identity after losing his identical twin brother.

Kate's Club 205
Kate Atwood was only 12 when her mother
died of breast cancer. As a young adult, Kate
offers grieving kids the resources she wishes
she'd had during that difficult time.

Finding the Perfect Niche:
Creative Entrepreneurs

Free Shoes 209
Missing out on winning $1 million put
Amazing Race contestant Blake Mycoskie
on an unexpected path to doing good.

The Birth of the Zingo Nation 213
PX Head made a terrible choice to drink and
drive, leading to the death of a friend. Now
this young man is saving lives and making the
most of his incredible second chance.

Smooth Mooove 217
Downsized corporate executive Adrienne
Simpson finds a new new niche in helping
seniors move.

The Do-Good Junkie 221
Recovering addict James Burgett discovers a
better high—recycling discarded computers
and helping others rehabilitate their lives.

Making Money for Fun 226
Cameron Johnson tells how he made his first
$1 million—by age 15.

Sweet Opportunity 230
Michele Hoskins turned an old family recipe
into a successful business—and now she
teaches others how to do the same.

Tying on Success 234
Shep and Ian Murray leave the corporate life
behind to make their fortune in ties.

Big, Beautiful, and Bodacious 239
Frustrated with fashion for women their size,
cousins Barb Wilkins and Lorna Ketler open
their own boutique and encourage women to
love themselves just the size they are.

Abundance on Aisle 6 243
From debtor to donor: how Tessa Greenspan
rejects bankruptcy and finds spiritual and
financial growth.

Power Tools 247
Barbara K, home fix-it diva, learns from
business setbacks and perseveres in her
desire to empower women do-it-yourselfers.

Closing Thoughts 252

What's Possible!

Daryn Kagan

Welcome to a world where just about anything is possible! If you have big dreams or huge obstacles to overcome, you've come to the right place. Or maybe you just love stories that make your heart go zing!

After more than 20 years in television news, I realized that's exactly what I loved. It's very important to be informed, and there's a lot of serious news that needs to be reported. But there are also many people doing amazing things that are worth reporting. Those are my favorite stories, and there are not enough outlets for them to be told.

Is it possible that a journalist who spent her entire career reporting doom and gloom could come to a point where she realized that what she spent her days covering on traditional newscasts was completely at odds with her optimistic view of the world? Is it really possible that I walked away from a successful news career to dedicate my life to telling inspirational stories?

It's not only possible, it's my own inspiring story, a story that begins with my getting fired. Well, OK, not fired exactly, but rather shown the proverbial door.

The Exit

"I know that your contract is up at the end of the year and I wanted you to know that we won't be renewing it." That was the big boss informing me that my 12-year CNN career was coming to an end. It was the best thing CNN ever did for me.

Let's be clear: CNN did some great things for me over those 12 years. First they plucked me out of Phoenix television and helped me transform from a local news reporter to a national sports anchor.

Three years later they moved me to the news desk where I covered everything from war to the Oscars. I traveled across Africa with Bono and then-U.S. Treasury Secretary Paul O'Neill. During that almost nine-year span, my home base was the CNN news desk. As the late-morning news anchor, I had a front-row seat on the roller coaster of the world. It meant that I was on the air as the second plane hit the World Trade Center on 9/11. It meant that I could be sitting there interviewing a senator, only to be told in my ear, "Wrap. We have Tom Cruise on the phone. Interview him about his Golden Globe nomination." Or "The King of Spain is on the phone. Interview him for three minutes." Then while interviewing the king, I could be told through my earpiece, "We think we have a school shooting in Colorado; you need to switch to the police department representative." For a news junkie it was the kind of professional challenge I craved. Not the kind of job you give up willingly.

That's why I needed the kick in the pants to leave. From the bottom of my heart, I can now say, "Thanks, Boss!"

The Hurt

Don't get me wrong. When I received the news that I was on my way out in January 2006, I didn't go pirouetting out of the boss's office singing, "Wahoo! I'm so happy I'm going to go transform the world with inspirational news!" No, hardly. I definitely had to go through the process of what I call "Feeling the Feel."

Trust me, turning 43 and not having a tie to anything in the world that I could see at that moment did not feel good. On top of that CNN had asked me to stay to finish out the last year of my contract. "I have no intention of taking you off the air," the boss added. Then he paused, "Well, I don't think I do. I'll let you know." So every day I went to work,

I delivered the news to millions around the world, handled the Israeli-Lebanese conflict, the Iraq war—really heady stuff—and tossed to weather with a smile. All the while I never knew if that day was my last day. Yes, that part wasn't so fun either.

It's important to remember that as you read the inspiring stories in this book. Very few people skip the hurt, the sadness, the tears, or even the fear. The story begins when you work through those feelings and decide, "OK, what's next?"

Elimination

My first step in "What's next?" was what would *not* be next. I made a decision that was shocking to many. I decided I was done with traditional TV news. To some it seemed like I was walking away from a boyfriend who had been good to me. I can see that. I loved my 20-plus years in news. I loved telling stories and live TV. It's much like being an emergency room doctor. You show up each day with a set of skills and you have no idea what's going to come rolling through the door. It's really intense for the few hours you're on the air. Then, just like that, you're done. Come back the next day and do it all over again.

> The story begins when you work through those feelings and decide, "OK, what's next?"

Yes, I loved all that—and I still do.

But I could see that both the news business and I were changing. Technology means jobs are disappearing. With all the ways to access information, how much longer will stations need an anchor delivering the news? And there is no doubt that TV executives like their talent younger and cheaper.

That's the main reason I never asked why. I never asked the boss why he wasn't renewing my contract. What was he going to say? "We want someone younger. We can get someone cheaper." Two facts of life: I wasn't getting younger and I sure didn't want to get cheaper!

Before you yell "Lawsuit!" or "That's not fair!" I must share that a bigger factor was at work. When I look back I realize I wasn't being completely true to myself by reporting all that depressing news. Newsrooms are pretty cynical places—the old "if it bleeds it leads" philosophy rules. Again, I think it's important to report hard news stories. And it's important to be informed. But in my personal life I was becoming someone who chose more and more to focus on the positive. We all make mini newscasts about life in our mind. We pick a point of view, whether it's "the world is a dangerous place," "the world is a bad place," or "the world is a good place," and then we go around collecting stories to support that idea.

So even before the boss booted me, had I been honest with myself, I was becoming someone who wanted to stress the positive.

Once I did get the boot, how was I supposed to find a job as an inspirational reporter? Being seen by the public and the news business as a serious, hard-news anchor who was on CNN for a long time was now an obstacle I would have to overcome. To have my professional life reflect my personal beliefs, I would have to make a big shift. I knew I could reinvent myself because I had done it before. That's how I made it to CNN.

Reinvention

Come to think of it, just getting to CNN is a wild *What's Possible!* story. In the early '90s I was working at a local TV station in Phoenix. The unspoken rule there was if you were blonde you were a news anchor. If you were brunette you were a reporter. Take a look at the cover of this book and you'll instantly know what my job was. Simply put, I did a lot of reporting. That wasn't entirely bad. The station covered everything, so in my 5½ years there I learned how to tell stories. Murders, floods, trials, riots, plane crashes, political scandals—I reported from every corner of the beautiful state of Arizona. I went live from helicopters. I went live from the bottom of meteor craters. I dug my high heels into the melting pavement covering record high 122°F heat.

It was a great experience, but like most local news reporters, I wanted to be one of the anchors. In local news markets the anchors are paid more money and get a billboard along the town's interstate. At the time that's what I thought was important.

So each time there would be a small anchor opening, I would go into the news director and ask for a shot.

"Oh, Daryn," he would sigh, not believing we were doing this dance again. "I've explained to you so many times. In television there's just this 'it' factor. Some people have it; some people don't. Clearly you don't. If you work really hard, one day you'll be a very good news reporter here in Phoenix. But why would you dream of being more than that?"

His rejection broke my ambitious heart and yet made me more determined. "I know, I'll show him," I would tell myself. "I'll just go become an even better reporter. Then he'll love me and give me a chance."

You can guess how this part of the story ends. I worked my butt off as a reporter. And, yes, I did improve. But, no, I never did get my chance to anchor the news in Phoenix.

I couldn't see it at the time, but that rejection was serving me. It inspired me to question what I really wanted to be doing. That was the first time I asked myself, "What are the stories I like the best?" The answer then was sports stories. I grew up with an older brother and a father who were both sports fans. Dad took us to all kinds of events: USC football, UCLA track meets, Lakers games, and—at the risk of dating myself—the Los Angeles Rams (when they *were* the Los Angeles Rams, playing NFL games in the Coliseum before they moved south to Orange County and ultimately to St. Louis).

> "Women don't do sports," he informed me. "Men won't watch women doing sports."

Back I went, marching into that news director's office. "I want to do sports," I told my news director.

"Women don't do sports," he informed me. "Men won't watch women doing sports."

No, this wasn't the Stone Age, more like 1993. And I knew this news director was wrong. Well, maybe he was right that I didn't have that special "it" factor to succeed as a news anchor, but all you had to do was flip the channels to see that women were coming on strong in the world of sports. Robin Roberts was climbing the ladder at ESPN, and Hannah Storm was anchoring for CNN Sports. I knew there was opportunity out there. All I needed was a shot, even if it took some extra work on my part.

The first step was learning how to be a sports anchor. I saw my chance when the station started a weekend morning newscast. Back I went into the news director's office. "You know that new show? I want to be the sportscaster for that," I declared.

"That show doesn't have a sportscaster job," the news director said.

"I know," I replied. "I made up the job and gave it to myself! No competition!"

Of course, this news director had no interest in my becoming a sportscaster, especially since I had worked so hard to improve my reporting that I was now his top reporter. Also, in the news business if you work weekends, you get two days off during the middle of the week. This was not going to work for this news director. "No," he tried to shut me down. "You're my best reporter. I'm not giving you Monday and Tuesday off so that you can learn how to do sports."

"What if I do it on my own time?" I countered.

"You're going to work seven days a week?" he asked, amazed.

"How about this," I offered. "We'll try it for a month. If you think I'm really bad at sports or falling down on my reporting duties, you can pull me off."

It's really hard for a boss to turn you down when you offer to do something for free. We had a deal. And I had inside information. Having worked for this man for more than three years, I at least knew how he worked. He was a family man. There was no way he was waking up weekend mornings and watching this show. I could do the sports gig for as long as I needed to. I did it for a year and a half. Yes, for a year and a half I worked the weeknight shift covering the lead story for the 10 p.m. news. Weekends I woke up just after 4 a.m. to come in and do sports, learn how to cut highlights, the whole bit.

It's a Haircut?!

It would be nice if I could tell you all it took was hard work and dedication to take me to the next level. But it wouldn't be the whole story. I worked like crazy that last year while also sending out resume tapes trying to get another job. Nothing. Zip. Zilch. I was applying for both reporting and news jobs. I didn't have a single nibble. And no one would tell me why.

Finally one of my best friends at the station, Cater Lee, offered me a lifeline. Cater was, and still is, blonde and—you guessed it—the main anchor at the station. She is also very talented, a hard worker, and a tremendous friend. "My agent, Jean Sage, is working with some women doing sports. You should send her a tape," Cater offered.

This sounded like an excellent idea. Like most people working in TV news, I, too, was working with an agent, but he wasn't giving me any constructive advice, let alone new job offers.

"But I have to tell you," Cater warned. "Jean is very blunt."

I gave Cater that "You have to be kidding me" look. As my good friend she knew that I was living through one of those life nadir moments. I was working seven days a week, couldn't find a new job, and my current boyfriend had dumped me. There was nothing Jean Sage could say to me that was going to hurt my feelings.

So I sent her a tape. She, too, warned me that she tells it like it is. I just never expected her advice. "You're actually very good," she assured me. "But you need to update your look."

"Update my look?" I asked.

"Yes," she said. "Cut your hair. You'll be shocked how fast you get a job."

Let me break into this story for a moment with some hair information. Even though I wear my hair smooth and straight now, I actually have very curly hair. And at that time I was wearing it naturally curly down past my shoulders. I would instruct you to picture an '80s big hairstyle, only I don't want to hurt your brain.

I couldn't believe this was the advice for which I had been so hungry.

"A haircut?" I asked somewhat incredulously. "Lady, I went to Stanford, I've won Emmy Awards, I'm working seven days a week, and you're telling me it's a haircut?!"

"That's it," she assured me. "Cut your hair, but be ready to go because that next job will come quickly."

I had nothing to lose and no other advice to follow. I hung up the phone, went directly to the local salon, and went from big '80s curly to short pixie.

Two weeks later CNN hired me as a sports anchor—the two things the news director in Phoenix told me I would never do: sports and anchor.

I promise you won't find anyone else in this book who had to overcome the obstacle of not being blonde.

Dreams Come True

Talk about dreams coming true. If you're going to do sports, the network level is the place to do it.

CNN sent me to cover everything from college football to the NFL, NBA, and international figure skating. Someone had to stand next to Troy Aikman while he was wearing nothing more than a towel and interview him in the Dallas Cowboys locker room. Someone had to follow Michelle Kwan to interview her as she stepped off the ice in Russia. That someone was me. It was a wonderful three-year run.

Just as that contract was ending, CNN hired a new president, Rick Kaplan. He called me into his office. "This sports thing is good, but have you ever thought about doing news?" he asked.

"Sure," I explained. "Every day that I went to work for 8½ years. I just made this sports thing up."

"Well," he mused, "I'm thinking about making you one of my news anchors, but I only like anchors who have reporting experience. Do you?"

"You bet!" I beamed. "That's all I was ever allowed to do for 5½ years in Phoenix. I was never allowed anywhere near an anchor desk!"

That was the first time I could see that sometimes a struggle or a particular dream not coming true was actually preparing me for an even bigger dream. All those times I cried for not having a shot at anchoring in Phoenix, I could never have imagined that I would become a news anchor for CNN! At the time that possibility was beyond my wildest imagination.

Off I went to the news desk. To the late morning slot, 9 a.m. to noon EST. Technically this time slot isn't as prestigious as the earlier 7 to 9 a.m. slot, but I loved it. The world's day is just getting started by late morning. It's when news starts breaking, when anything can happen. You have to strap in and go for the breaking-news ride.

Because the slot wasn't as high profile as the prime time New York-based shows, I had to talk my way into going on assignment. But that was nothing for me after being told all those years in Phoenix that I didn't have "it."

I covered the Washington, D.C.-area sniper. I was on hand for the crash of Space Shuttle *Columbia*. I saw war in the Middle East with the invasion of Iraq. And on the complete opposite side of the news spectrum, I covered the battleground of the Oscars' red carpet.

All those were incredible professional experiences, but not the ones that I found the most satisfying.

On the set my last day at CNN, September 1, 2006. My smile reflects gratitude for an amazing 12-year run at "The World's News Leader" and excitement and nervousness for the next chapter that awaited me.

On the red carpet at the Oscars, February 2004. This was always one of my favorite events to cover. Not because of the glitz and glam—rather, going live meant having to be ready to interview any star who passed by. The ultimate pop quiz.

Covering the beginning of the Iraq war, March 2003. My beat was anchoring from Kuwait City and covering Kuwait, the neighboring country Saddam Hussein had invaded and attacked 10 years earlier. That's one of many missiles that landed in and around the capital city.

All along, I loved the stories that made my heart go zing!

I even created a segment on my show called "Your Spirit." My argument was that every Friday we would have on a movie critic, Mr. Moviephone. He was great and a lot of fun. But I'd bet more people do something with their spiritual lives over the weekend than go to a movie. Yet traditional media doesn't cover that. It's as if spiritual matters don't exist. If traditional media does cover religion, it's about molestation and church leaders. Don't get me wrong. I think it's important to cover those stories. But for most people, I think religion and spirituality are about finding meaning in life, improving themselves, their families, and the world. Sometimes a spiritual act is simply doing something good in the world. Those are great stories.

Again, just as in Phoenix, I did these stories on my own time. Little did I know I was getting ready for the next chapter of my life.

Inspiration

After 12 years at CNN, I was now facing the big blank slate of my life. CNN was coming to a close, and I knew I no longer had the passion to go after another traditional news job. But what else was there?

So many people are looking for inspiration. "I don't know what I want to do," they'll say. If there is one thing I wish I had known at the beginning of this next chapter in my life, it is that inspiration comes in pieces. It doesn't just drop on your desk all at once like a pile of bricks. When most people don't see it all at once, they think it's not there. I had to learn that inspiration comes in pieces and that it can come from the most unlikely sources.

How about this: I got the original spark to launch an inspirational news website while looking at a site dedicated to war coverage. Yes, war! It doesn't get much less "feel good" than war stories.

For much of 2006 Yahoo! had a page dedicated to a man named Kevin Sites. Kevin is a longtime war correspondent. I knew him from the days he worked at CNN. He also reported for NBC. The Yahoo! page was called "Kevin Sites in the Hot Zone: One Man. One Year. A World of Conflict."

I found it fascinating that the Internet was expanding to create individual pages for reporters on a single topic. I couldn't help daydreaming.

What would my one year and one page be focused on? While I had covered war, it certainly wouldn't be that. It wasn't my passion. That's when it came to me: inspirational stories! The ones I loved more than anything. Why not "Daryn Kagan in the Inspirational Zone: One Woman. One Year. One Wonderful Feeling"?

It was the first time I was excited about anything since I had received the "you're outta here" news in January.

I was so excited, in fact, that I actually tried to give my idea away! I figured if Yahoo! was excited about Kevin Sites and his Hot Zone, surely they would be excited about me. I managed to talk my way into a Yahoo! executive's office and made what I figured was a brilliant pitch. "Visitors get so much when they come to Yahoo! You can get your news headlines, sports, stocks, and weather forecast. But where is the 'Yahoo!' in Yahoo!?" I asked. It seemed straightforward to me. A no-brainer. What a basic for the brand. A user should be able to feel "Yahoo!" by visiting Yahoo!

> Another important lesson: Don't take someone's blindness to your vision as a personal rejection.

The executive just stared back at me. Apparently he didn't see the same basic brilliance. That's OK. Another important lesson: Don't take someone's blindness to your vision as a personal rejection. It's just more information. You're meant to move on. But where?

It turns out that I received the next bit of inspiration from someone who has been one of my most brilliant business advisors, my younger sister, Kallan. She suggested I create the website myself, then build the inspiring brand into books and broadcasting.

This time I was the reluctant respondent. I didn't know anything about starting and running a company, let alone the Internet.

Yet as time went on, the idea grew on me—mostly because by doing it myself I wouldn't have to wait for some executive to pick me, to decide if I had "it." This time it was just a matter of getting started myself.

What's in a Name?

From the moment I decided to head off into these uncharted waters, the most amazing things started happening. Like many of the people you will meet in this book, I found I could tell I was on the right track with this crazy idea because everyone and everything I needed just started showing up.

The first order of business was picking a name for the website. With 12 years on national TV under my belt, I figured one of my strongest assets was my unusual name. There aren't many women named Daryn. The name for my website was a simple choice: DarynKagan.com.

Many of you may have registered a domain name before. I certainly had not. I learned that it's a simple process: You go to any number of websites, plug in the name you want to use, and for less than $10 you own the name. There's only one problem—if someone grabbed that name before you did. That's what happened to me. I typed in "d-a-r-y-n-k-a-g-a-n.-c-o-m."

"That domain name has been taken," my computer screen told me.

"But how can that be?" I wondered. I also figured it would be no big deal to straighten out. I just needed to explain the problem to the domain company. This would just take one phone call. Oh, how little I knew about the Internet! I laugh now.

"Clearly there has been some mistake," I explained to the person on the other end of the phone. "This guy who registered DarynKagan.com down in Florida is not me. We need to do something about that."

I didn't get the response I was expecting. The customer rep explained that it's called cybersquatting. People register names they think someone will want, hoping to sell the names back at a really high price. It could cost tens or hundreds of thousands of dollars to get my name back.

I hung up thinking that was not the response I wanted to hear and that there had to be a better way. Then came yet another drop of inspiration.

"Let's just test this out," I challenged myself. "What is this website supposed to be about anyway? Love? Or hate? Let's just see."

I had the person's email address and decided to write him.

"Dear Mr. Boone," I wrote. "Thank you for thinking of me when you went to register domain names. But now the time has come for DarynKagan.com to go back to its rightful owner, which, of course, would be me.

"I've talked with the domain company, and it's no big deal for you to transfer ownership. Three clicks and you can hand my name back to me."

That is, in fact, true. But the owner of the domain name must be willing to hand it over.

My email didn't mention money; I didn't mention lawyers; I didn't even say what I wanted to do with the website.

Thomas Boone called me the very next day. He's an artist in Boca Raton, Florida. He emailed some pictures of his work. Of course I told him how nice his work was. We eventually got around to the topic of DarynKagan.com. "Why didn't you ever register your name?" he asked.

"I never had anything I wanted to do with it," I explained. "But now I do."

Then Thomas Boone became pensive. "Why do you think I have your name?" he wondered aloud. "Why do you think out of everyone in the world who could have registered your name, I have it?"

"Uh, I don't know," I replied. Honestly I was starting to get a bit nervous, especially as he paused. Silence. Then he said, "I think I know why I have your name."

"Why is that?" I asked.

"I think I was meant to hold on to it so that no one else would take advantage of you," he explained.

Wow. "Well, can I have it back?" I asked ever so politely.

"Yes, you can have it back," he answered.

Just like that, that night Thomas Boone did the three clicks it took to transfer ownership to me. Not a dime changed hands. No lawyers. Nothing.

I called the domain company just to make sure that we were doing everything the right way. The techie on the other end of the line couldn't believe what he was hearing. "I hope you appreciate that this *never* happens this way," he wanted me to know. It was just the beginning of so many wonderful things that happened to launch me on my new pathway of delivering inspirational stories to the world.

Great! How Can We Get It Done?

As I moved closer and closer to leaving CNN, I started sharing with colleagues my plan to launch DarynKagan.com. Friends were interested in my next move. And I knew there was a lot of talent around the building that could give me guidance since I had so much to learn. That included learning to shoot my own stories. Of course, when you report at the network level, you have the most talented crews who go with you to do the stories, shoot the video, and record the sound. It's important to have professionals because there is a very specific way of shooting video so that it can be edited into a smooth-looking piece. It can't look like a home video.

But now I was scaling down to what we like to call a one-man band. Just as in small-market television, I knew there would be times when I would have to take my own camera and shoot the story myself. I needed some shooting lessons and I knew just whom to ask.

Dan Young was my shooter when I traveled in Africa in 2002, covering the trip of U2's Bono and U.S. Treasury Secretary Paul O'Neill. He was the sunniest of souls, always eager to help and to figure out a challenge. No matter what someone would ask, Dan's response was, "Great! How can we get that done?!" And he always appeared delighted and honored that you would ask him for help.

Shortly after our trip to Africa, Dan was promoted to CNN chief videographer. Management, Grand Poobah, Big Cheese. He was in charge of every CNN videographer, but it didn't change him a bit. He was still the great guy whom anyone could always ask for help.

"I know," I thought. "I'll ask Dan for shooting lessons!" Great idea, but it never happened. Summer 2006, three weeks before I left CNN, Dan suddenly came down with leukemia. A week later he died. There are no words to describe how shocking it was. Vibrant, healthy, nonstop-energy Dan dead at 47? It devastated the network. This wonderful man and friend who spent more than half his life working at CNN was gone way too soon.

Dan's funeral was standing room only. And that was in the extra spillover room. There was no church that could hold all the love that showed up for Dan that day. As I looked over at his wife, his young son, and his twin brother, my heart ached for them.

The next day in the CNN newsroom, I ran into another longtime CNN shooter, Dave Haeberlin. We hugged. We shared memories of Dan. Then Dave asked me, "What's this project you're working on? Tell me about your website."

I told him about DarynKagan.com and got a brilliant idea. I would ask Dave for shooting lessons! Plan B! "Hey, Dave," I said. "I could actually use your help. I could use some shooting lessons."

Then one of the most incredible things happened. Without missing a beat, Dave looked at me and said, "Dan took care of that."

What? Surely Dave had misunderstood me. I'd never had a chance to explain my website to Dan, let alone ask him for shooting lessons. How could he have taken care of it? But Dave insisted that that was exactly what Dan had done. Two weeks earlier he had written down a lesson plan explaining how to shoot a story so it could be edited into a nice piece. Dave emailed it to me.

Sure enough, it was line for line exactly the shooting lesson I needed from Dan! Through the words, through the excellent instruction, I could feel Dan looking back at me with that delighted twinkle in his eye, saying, "Great! We got it done!"

DarynKagan.com Launches

And so it went. Day after day little angels and helpers kept showing up to help me create DarynKagan.com as well as the next chapter of my career and life. On November 13, 2006, DarynKagan.com went online. If you haven't already checked it out, I hope you will. You'll find my daily webcast where I feature the story of the day. There are also 12 different buckets or categories: Animals, Artists, Business, Celebrities, Charity/ Nonprofit, Heroes, Kids, Over 60, Overcoming Obstacles, Sports, World Events, and a late addition: The Love Bucket, which is just great love stories.

> It's amazing what happens when you don't put a label on something, how it can be there for people of many political and spiritual beliefs to enjoy.

An interesting thing happened when I was creating the site. As I would tell people about it, they would get excited and invariably burst out, "Ooh! Ooh! I have a story!" That was another piece of the puzzle that I needed to pick up. People aren't just hungry for these kinds of stories—they also want to participate. That's why there's a big box on every page of DarynKagan.com that says, "Tell Me Your Story!" About 70 percent of the stories on the website now come from folks writing in. Some even produce the stories themselves.

I also quickly learned that stories have a magical unifying quality. I heard from leftist environmentalists saying, "Thank you for creating a site for us!" At the same time I heard from right wing evangelical Christians saying, "Thank you for creating a site for us!" To all of them and everyone in between I say, "You're welcome!" The stories are for everyone. It's amazing what happens when you don't put a label on something, how it can be there for people of many political and spiritual beliefs to enjoy.

The website was only up and running a few weeks when it became apparent this project would soon grow bigger than just the Internet. I started hearing from professionals in the book world. "Have you thought about doing a book?" they would ask.

Yes, I had thought about it, but a book is a lot of work, and it was all I could do to keep up with the demands of the newborn baby website. Again just the right people showed up to help make that part of the dream a reality. Writer Bill Beausay of Columbus, Ohio, was a cheerleader from the beginning. He's been the locomotive of this operation, keeping it going when I felt overwhelmed, helping to conduct some of the interviews, trading drafts back and forth with me, keeping me on schedule.

Lisa Berkowitz, an editor with Meredith Books, contacted me and spent a good hour on the phone hashing out ideas without any promise of getting a book deal out of it. Without each of them, you and I wouldn't be sitting here having this book experience.

There are all sorts of inspiring stories on DarynKagan.com, but Lisa helped me focus this first book on stories from Overcoming Obstacles. It makes sense. Those are the most popular. I've included a few in this book that have appeared on the website. There were some gems that I simply couldn't leave out—kind of like hearing your favorite song in concert and wanting it on the album too. Most of the stories, however, are fresh and new for this collection.

Looking at the list of what people in this book have faced in their lives—losing a loved one, cancer, legal troubles, weight issues, corporate layoffs—you could think, "Whoa! So much for an uplifting book." That's true if you stop there. The truth is, stuff happens—it happens to a lot of us. The inspiration comes when you read about what folks have done with what has happened to them. That's the ride I hope you take with me as you turn the pages.

If your heart swells, a smile comes to your face, a tear sometimes comes to your eye, then this book will have achieved its purpose. If the folks in this book make you take a second look at your own dreams and believe that incredible things are possible, then all the better.

Part 1

Defying the Odds: Overcoming Physical Challenges

No Excuses

Scott Rigsby,
double amputee and history-making Ironman triathlete

"Scott Rigsby, you are an Ironman!" The noise and cheering was deafening as I crossed the finish line with minutes to spare at the Ironman Triathlon in Kona, Hawaii. That magnificent moment in October 2007 seemed a lifetime away from the day nine years before when I begged a doctor to amputate my remaining leg.

My journey began in 1986. I was 18 years old, working for a landscaping company in South Georgia. I was riding in the bed of a pickup truck that was pulling a trailer full of equipment. I guess in hindsight I should have seen how dangerous this was, but I was carefree and irresponsible.

In a freak accident, we were hit by a semitruck. The collision sent me skidding down 328 feet. My flesh ripped away from my body as I ended up wedged under the 6,000-pound trailer with my right foot severed at the ankle. Thankfully, the weight of the trailer acted as a tourniquet on my leg, keeping me from bleeding to death right there. It was a hopeless predicament because there was no machinery within miles that could possibly pull the wreckage off my body.

Then, in what I can only describe as a miracle, a tow truck arrived out of nowhere and performed the impossible: It lifted the trailer off me.

Keep in mind, I was far out in the country. There were no tow trucks for miles around, much less one big enough for this job. Eyewitnesses at the scene told me that they'd never heard of the tow truck company or the driver before or since. It was as if Roma Downey from *Touched by an Angel* showed up. Of all the miracles in my life, that was No. 1.

I should have been thankful because I could have or should have been dead. My right leg was badly mangled and had to be amputated that day. Trust me on this: Nothing can prepare you to look down and see your leg gone below your knee, no matter what the circumstances are. I felt fortunate that I still had my other leg, and I was determined that one day I would walk again.

But the obstacles in my way were more than I could have ever imagined. They included 25 surgeries to fix my remaining battered leg and 12 years as a professional patient. I don't want to harp on the difficulties I encountered, so let me just say that my leg never healed properly and was constantly inflamed and infected.

After facing incredible odds and losing the battle, I knew it was time to let go. I was 30 years old by that time, and life wasn't turning out like I had thought it would. I had become a bitter, angry, and resentful person.

There's very little that I haven't faced on this comeback trail, including excruciating pain, severe depression, alcoholism, painkiller addiction, and a constant urge to end it all. It felt like watching a sad movie with a wrenching breakup. My breakup was losing my old life.

Fortunately for me this turned out to be a pity party for one. My family and friends were not having it. Twelve years into this drama centered on saving my leg, I decided I was done being a professional patient. I went to the doctor and said, "I want my life back and I was wondering if you could help me out. I want you to take off the other leg."

It's not as easy as all that. I had to go through a series of psychological tests proving that I wasn't crazy and knew what I was asking.

I did. I was asking to say goodbye to surgery and medical treatment and hello to a world of modern prosthetics that make amazing things possible. Within six weeks from the time I had the second amputation, I was running on my new prosthetic legs.

Beyond running I discovered the world of triathlons. I started with the South Carolina Half Ironman. That means a 1.2-mile swim, a 56-mile bike ride, topped off by a 13.1-mile run. For the swim, I go with just what is left of my legs. For the bike, I have special prostheses that actually clip into the bike pedals where you would expect my feet to be. For the run, I have these very cool legs that look like giant spatulas.

So far, I've become the first double amputee to complete an Olympic-distance triathlon, a half marathon, and a full marathon. But my big dream was to complete the big daddy of all triathlons—The Ironman: a 2.4-mile swim, a 112-mile bike ride, and a full 26.2-mile marathon. I wanted to push the boundaries of what people thought a physically challenged athlete could do.

> I had to tell myself to stop listening to the negative thoughts and to divide the challenge into what I could and couldn't control.

I took my first shot at the full Ironman distance in June 2007 in Coeur d'Alene, Idaho. I started with one of my best swims ever, even though the weather was so bad that day that the racers were given the option of skipping that portion. The bad weather did catch up with me during the bike ride. I wiped out at mile 17. For me, that doesn't mean just falling off the bike. I actually can't because even in a spill, the clips of my prostheses keep me attached. So I flipped over the handlebars and landed on my back and shoulders.

I got back on the bike, not realizing how badly I had injured myself. I actually had pieces of vertebrae floating around in my back. It all caught up with me halfway through the 26-mile run. They had to take me away in an ambulance. That was just about the only way they could have gotten me to leave the course without crossing the finish line.

It put me in a terrible position to do my final preparation for the biggest Ironman of them all in Kona, Hawaii, in October 2007. I wasn't able to get in the kind of training I needed in those remaining summer months.

The pressure was certainly on. My bank account was empty. This was going to be my one last shot to make history and attract the kind of sponsorship I needed to train full-time. If I failed, I would just be another guy with a big dream that didn't come true.

The challenges started right away with the swim portion of the race: 1,800 pumped-up, elite athletes plunging into the Pacific Ocean all at once. I guess I shouldn't have been surprised that almost immediately I got kicked in my right eye. It was pretty swollen by the time I emerged from the water 1½ hours later. It didn't bother me too much, though, because I was jazzed that I had done so well. This was only the fourth time I had swum in the ocean, and at one hour 28 minutes, it was my best time ever.

It was time to peel off my wet suit and put on the biking legs. The bike portion also went well until I hit mile 78, where I encountered the most unbelievable headwinds. Imagine going up a steep driveway and deciding to stop pedaling. It felt at times like I was going backwards even though I was giving it my all to go forward.

I really became concerned because if I kept going like this for the next 34 miles, I would have no energy left for the marathon. Even more than the physical challenges, the thoughts in your own head are what beat you in the Ironman, so I made a vital decision. I just had to tell myself to stop listening to the negative thoughts and to divide the challenge into what I could and couldn't control.

I couldn't control those darned headwinds, but I could control my heart rate. I reached down and changed the gear on my bike. I focused on my cadence, an easy spin, and when the winds let up a little bit, I was back at my normal pace.

The biggest challenge with the run portion was the clock. The race officials don't give you forever to finish the course. It all shuts down at midnight, 17 hours after the start. About mile 10 one of the officials informed me that I would have to pick up my pace or I wasn't going to make the cutoff. This meant no time for walking; I'd have to run the entire 26.2 miles.

I can honestly say during the last three miles of the run I was in the most intense pain I have ever felt in my life. Giant pools of sweat had collected where my legs meet my prostheses. The skin there had moved beyond blisters. It was more like big sheets of raw skin rubbing up against the prostheses.

If I was going to quit, this would have been the place. To keep my mind off the pain, I started thinking about how I had been training for this moment for a year and a half. I thought about my older brother who is intellectually and developmentally disabled and has never walked a day in his life. I thought about all the naysayers who didn't believe I could do this. I thought about all the people who sacrificed, gave me services for free, donated money, loved me just to get me to this moment.

That was the juice that propelled me over the Ironman finish line 16 hours 42 minutes and 46 seconds after I started. I beat the cutoff by just over 17 minutes.

That moment was unlike anything I've ever experienced. The cheering was deafening. People were screaming, yelling, and crying. It was so great to hear Mike Reilly, the voice of Ironman, announce, "Scott Rigsby, you are an Ironman!"

The price of my personal victory was higher than I expected. I did so much damage to the ends of my legs that I had to use a wheelchair for many days afterward. My legs were too raw and swollen to put on my prostheses.

And yet I want to do the Ironman again! People call me a physically challenged athlete, but I'm really an athlete who has some physical challenges. The athlete in me wants to go back next year and compete just like everybody else. I'm spending the year training and refining the prostheses to minimize the challenges that I had in '07.

I want to inspire people to go for their dreams. I want them to see what's possible even when people tell you there's no way it can be done, that it has never been done before. Most folks may never want to do an Ironman, but no matter what their dream is, there is no excuse not to go for it.

Not having legs is no excuse. Neither is having no guts. My story shows the biggest barrier is what you tell yourself in your head and how much will you have in your heart.

For more on Scott Rigsby go to scottrigsby.com.

Daryn's Takeaways

. . . .

During our interview Scott said, "It's amazing how far you can go if you let go of something that's not serving you anymore." In Scott's case that was his leg! Not only did he have to let go of a piece of his body, but he also had to let go of caring about what most people would think of his decision. Scott knew what was best for him. By letting go of his leg, he not only improved his health and lifestyle, he put himself in a position to better serve and inspire others—and to find new joy and purpose in life.

Is there something you are holding on to in your life that most people would think you are nuts to release? Could letting go actually improve your life?

It's Not About the Sculptures

Bill Montgomery,
91-year-old blind sculptor

The day I went blind was the day I finally began to see. It happened just as I was turning 80. Just when I thought my life was washed up, things started getting very interesting.

My art is my love, my passion. And it's something I didn't learn to do until I went blind.

Don't feel sorry for me because my eyes don't work. I'm one of the happiest people you'll ever meet. Why don't I just sit around like so many old people I know and be bored and talk about stool softeners and medical conditions? Because very late in life I found out that what you get in life is pretty much a choice.

I believe in being happy, joyous, and free. I'm a cage rattler: I feel like I'm in my twenties or thirties. Most of my good friends are in their twenties and thirties. I have action going on around me 24 hours a day! I'm so blessed that I can meet thrilling young people and talk about baseball, movies, theater, restaurants, and museums. Many of the older people around where I live think I'm a crackpot because I wear funny hats and pajamas and have friends that laugh and smile a lot. Every year of my life is more exciting than the last.

Before you think I'm some freak of good nature, let me share more of my story. It's taken just about every one of my then-80 years to get to this place. Even before the blindness set in, I had my share of challenges.

In 1983 I came face-to-face with the fact that I was an alcoholic. Several years later I had to watch my wife, my lifelong lover, partner, and friend—my everything—disintegrate before my eyes as she struggled with Parkinson's disease. She died after a long battle. Then my beloved grandson Tommy was killed in a tragic car accident. And finally, 12 years ago, I suddenly lost my sight due to glaucoma.

You have to go back to 1949 to find out why I started turning to alcohol. That's the year I moved my family from New York to Atlanta. I had been a buyer for Bloomingdale's department store and went to work in retail when I arrived in Atlanta. Although I was traveling quite a bit, my family meant the world to me, and we were quite happy living in the South.

Honestly, though, I was not a very happy person. I had deep and persistent doubts about myself and felt that I was a fraud. I might laugh and smile on the outside, but on the inside I felt like I was worthless. I feared if people found out what I was really like they would hate me.

I suppose different people handle this inner split in different ways, but my solution was drinking. I was an alcoholic and a terribly insecure one at that.

I actually got my life back on October 2, 1983, when I started attending Alcoholics Anonymous meetings. That's where I discovered that it was possible for people to know me intimately and still love me. I was in my sixties at the time, but finding out that one simple fact totally rocked my world. I realized then that somebody, my higher power, had been walking by my side all my life.

Still I had no idea what was ahead of me. The biggest challenge was losing my wife. The loss crushed me. It seems today that people talk about soulmates like they're all over the place. But that was not my experience. My wife was a lifelong partner and in so many wonderful ways an extension of me. Losing my sweetheart was harder than anything I had ever experienced.

After her death I decided to take a long trip, a lifetime dream, and went to the Orient. On that trip I had some profound realizations. Among them, I realized that I didn't need anybody to make me happy.

Happiness isn't something that comes from outside: Happiness is something generated from within. And when I made that simple connection, everything changed for me.

I came back home and became very active in Alcoholics Anonymous, participating in four to eight meetings each week. I sponsored many people and felt that to some extent I was giving back to others in a way that could change lives. For the first time in my life I felt like I was being myself and being rewarded for it. Everything was awesome!

> Your life is a precious gift to others, and passing along your love of it is vital to long, happy living.

So you can imagine my surprise when in 1994 I was sitting in the middle of a busy intersection in Atlanta and suddenly went totally blind. Not only that, but I drove home six miles and parked safely in the driveway.

I joke about it now, but it was not funny.

Although I could still see shapes up close, losing most of my sight meant I could no longer do the things I enjoyed, such as drive, read, or travel on my own. I was climbing the walls with boredom. My physician suggested I enroll in a class where I could work with my hands. My son and daughter-in-law thought that a clay sculpting class was the answer.

I went along with the idea, and I'm glad I did. The first session was a nude study. You might think I'm a little beyond that, but it sure beat talking about nitroglycerin patches!

I had never thought of myself as an artist, but looking back I remember that during the Depression I did make some charcoal drawings at a local free museum in New York, and I did some whittling as a kid (my friends called me "Weedle"). But that isn't exactly a good pedigree for this kind of work. Nevertheless, I gave myself to it and began trying some new things.

After doing seven or eight pieces, I decided to do one of my grandson Tommy, whom I missed so much after his death. He loved basketball, so I sculpted him shooting the ball into the basket. Although it probably looked crude, I loved it. It was my boy Tommy.

I wanted to learn more. Let's be honest: It isn't so easy when you're blind as a bat. I decided that the only way I was really going to get anywhere with my sculpting gift was to study with the master, so that's what I did. My instructor, Teena Watson-Stern, recommended someone who changed my life: Lincoln Fox. He is a world-renowned sculptor from the beautiful mesa country of western Colorado. Lincoln taught me to "see with my fingers." He also taught me that every single piece I make must tell a story. And within each piece there should be a little part of me. I can't thank Lincoln enough for setting me free artistically, even though I was well into my eighties!

I had no plans of becoming a professional sculptor: I simply did it for myself. But in time people started buying my sculptures for thousands of dollars a piece. That's even mo' better!

The sculptures are my joy and my excitement, and they fill every day. What a fantastic life! I can honestly tell you that I don't miss my eyesight at all. But let me be clear: My great life really isn't about the art. It's not about working with clays and bronze and forms; it's about enjoying life and finding some way to express that enjoyment and pass it along to others.

Your life is a precious gift to others, and passing along your love of it is vital to long, happy living. Don't ever give up on this, even if others don't like it or aren't ready to receive it.

And remember, you can always pick yourself up, no matter how battered and broken and old you may be. You can begin again. You can choose to be happy, joyous, and free!

For more information go to sculpturebybill.com.

Daryn's Takeaways

I wish every one of you reading this book could spend an afternoon with Bill. His joy for life is infectious. Life took away his ability to see, but it also gave him his ability to produce amazing art. Bill wastes no time each day in bemoaning what's gone. He's too excited about celebrating what he has.

How much more would you get out of your day if you focused on all the gifts present in your life now rather than on what's gone or hasn't shown up yet?

Healing Myself, Healing the World

George Roundy,
advocate for the hungry

It's a happy day when you wake up weighing 370 pounds. Well, it's a happy day if it's the last day you'll be that way. I remember the day I decided that rather than lose the weight (which I always seemed to find again), I was going to release it forever. The fat was no longer serving me. But the real story is how I made $50,000 in the process and at the same time empowered a whole bunch of hungry people to end their hunger.

When you grow up fat with a last name like "Roundy," it's no joke. We Roundys were big in more ways than one. I have six sisters and two brothers. Several of us were afflicted with severe, nearly life-threatening obesity. My sister eventually lost 145 pounds on Weight Watchers and is healthy to this day. She inspired me in my journey.

My story was a little different. At my heaviest I weighed 370 pounds. I had a very poor relationship with food: I used it for stress relief, to kill bad feelings, to make myself feel better, to cure boredom, to celebrate, and so on. I tried many different kinds of diets but nothing worked. I always ran into the same challenges time and again. Those of you who struggle with obesity know what I mean. I came to believe that there was nothing that I could do about my weight and, worse, that I didn't really matter anyway, so losing weight would make no difference.

All was not doom and gloom in my life either. I have two wonderful sons, a beautiful wife, two grandchildren, a successful business, and many great things to live for. But resignation about my weight totally clouded my perspective.

It's always difficult to put your finger on what changes within you, but my 50th birthday was coming, and it definitely affected me. I didn't want to live the rest of my life with this extra weight.

The main change was attending a Landmark Leadership seminar where we were given the assignment to create a project that would touch the world. A seminar leader, Conde Rogers, came up with what I thought was a brilliant idea. Her goal was to lose 125 pounds and raise $25,000 in sponsorship money for a very special cause. Her cause was to buy a bicycle for every child attending a school for homeless children. Not only did she succeed, but she succeeded far beyond just giving away bicycles. How? She influenced the thinking of an important person: me!

From Conde's example I created the As We Heal, the World Heals project. My goal was to lose 150 pounds in one year and raise $50,000 in support of the Hunger Project, a movement founded 30 years ago to end hunger in sustainable ways. With 20,000 people dying every day from hunger, helping end the hunger cycle through supporting the Hunger Project became my "do or die trying" passion. This combination of healing myself and healing the world struck me as the perfect solution.

I chose the Hunger Project because it's making an impact on the world. Working at the grassroots level, it empowers people living in abject poverty and chronic hunger (primarily sub-Saharan Africa, South Asia, and Latin America) to end their own hunger and build lives of self-reliance.

As I began my own personal weight program, I was filled with so much fear. Would I run into the same obstacles that beat me before? What would I do then? How would my life change? How could I live without my security, my entertainment, my comfort? Did I deserve good health? Was I worth it?

While those fears swirled around my head, there were also signs that I was headed down the right path. I sent letters to everyone I knew telling them about my project. It was a pretty homespun operation, but it worked perfectly. Pledges and donations began flooding in from hundreds of people.

I found my thinking starting to shift about weight too. For instance, I discovered that words were very important in how I thought about beating my lifelong dependence on food. Rather than lose weight I decided to "release" the weight. I realized whenever I lost something I would always try to find it. That's certainly what always happened to me with my weight. Every pound I ever lost, I found again, and then some! However, by releasing the weight I was telling myself that the extra pounds no longer served me and they were free to go forever.

> Rather than lose weight I decided to "release" it, to tell myself that the extra pounds no longer served me and were free to go forever.

Of course, thinking itself doesn't burn a lot of calories, so I took some practical steps as well. I consulted with a physician, I hired a fitness coach, and I began eating better.

After all those years of crash diets, this time I decided not to use one. Instead I committed myself to eating smaller, more frequent, and healthy meals (to keep my metabolism high), and I did reflexology/energy work on various parts of my body that were focal points for my stress. Regular exercise (five to six times a week) became a priority as I built it into my lifestyle.

My fundraising focus also gave me new motivation to exercise. I remember one evening I arrived home late, about 11 p.m. I hadn't worked out that day, and it bothered me like never before. Then the thought struck me that there are women all over Africa at that moment who rise at 4:30 in the morning and work until 10 at night just to feed their families. Compared to the courage and commitment of these women, my 11 p.m. workout was a snap.

That was April 2006, and by April 2007 I had reached my goal: I had released 150 pounds and had attained the best shape of my life! With supporters pledging a certain dollar amount for every pound I released,

I raised $50,000 to help end world hunger. I guess you could say I was healed. In hindsight I can tell you that the hardest part of this whole project was the fear that consumed me when I first began. When I finally surrendered the fear and refused to allow it to rule me any longer, my life changed radically.

I'm now committed to a fundraiser every year until world hunger is wiped out. My next project is hiking from the Grand Canyon on Memorial Day 2008. I'm taking hundreds of people with me, and each will raise at least $1,000 for the Hunger Project. I feel that I've been given a second life to devote to something that is meaningful and enormous.

Let me urge you to learn a lesson from my experience. Whatever your biggest problem, your biggest obstacle, your biggest fear, use it to make a difference. Be creative in how you leverage your biggest pain to open your heart to the passion that lives deep down in each one of us.

You can contact The Hunger Project at thp.org or George at groundy@ecorridor.com.

Daryn's Takeaways

I love how George learned to use language to advantage. "Losing" weight didn't work for him because, as he says, he always felt compelled to go "find" it again, which he did too successfully.

But deciding it didn't "serve" him anymore brought about a big shift. He could now release it from his life.

What habits, feelings, or relationships no longer serve you in your life? What kind of amazing gifts would you have room to receive if you released that which no longer serves you?

Born with a Mark of Greatness

**Stephen Dale,
teenage musician and inspiration
for kids with facial differences**

When you look at my face, you'll see two eyes,
a nose, a mouth, and a large birthmark. It's been there since I was born
17 years ago. I'm as thankful for the birthmark as I am for my eyes, nose,
and mouth.

I believe I was born with a mark of greatness, and I'm dedicated
to teaching other kids with facial differences the same thing about
themselves.

My birthmark is impossible to miss. It's pink and reddish in color. It
covers the left half of my face, stretching down to my neck and chin and
a little bit over my Adam's apple. Doctors call it a port wine stain. It's
really a vascular malformation where the veins in that part of the skin are
dilated more than normal. Those veins become bigger and create the
red pigment.

I really noticed something was different about me when I was 5 or
6 years old. Kids in elementary school started making fun of me and made
me self-conscious.

It's true that kids can be cruel. I remember one boy who said, "You were so ugly when you were born, your mom spanked you on the face and that's how you got that red mark."

The mark was actually darker when I was younger. It has become lighter as I've grown. There's still no missing it, but when I was little it was almost like a mask I wore every day. I was taunted endlessly by kids who called me Red Face. I learned early on who my real friends were. Some kids would play with me, but when the other boys would come around, they would go with them and join in the taunts.

Somehow I knew how to turn this around. I decided there wasn't anything wrong or different about me. Instead I determined that the birthmark made me *better* than the other kids. I took it so far as to feel sorry for them. They must be jealous that I am special. How boring and sad it must be not to have a birthmark on their face and to look ordinary just like everyone else.

I never wished I didn't have my birthmark. All people have something that builds their character and turns them into the people they become. For me it was my birthmark. It has motivated me to work hard at everything I do, including pursuing my No. 1 passion: music.

My grandfather was a jazz musician in New Orleans who taught me just about everything I know. I started playing drums when I was only 4 years old. As long as I can remember, I would play for anybody who would listen.

A defining moment in my life came in seventh grade. I was new at the junior high school and entered the talent show. I was taking a really big chance that night because all the popular kids were in the show.

I walked on stage acting clumsy and shy. Then I started playing my drums very slowly and offbeat like it was the first time I ever played the drums. The cool kids didn't get my act at all and started to ask, "Who is this guy? Where did he come from?" When I heard them ask, "What's that on his face?" they almost laughed me off the stage.

But then I suddenly stopped playing and stood up. The crowd thought I was going to quit. Instead I reached into my back pocket, pulled out a handkerchief, and tied it around my head as a blindfold. I sat back down and played the best drum solo of my life. The crowd went crazy! When I was done, the entire gym gave me a standing ovation!

I won the talent show that night. A year later I was accepted into the New Orleans Center for Creative Arts (NOCCA). It's where the best young musicians in New Orleans go for training.

Now I've taken my music to the next step and have started to write songs. I actually wasn't that good when I started writing lyrics. I realize now it's because I was trying to copy what was on the radio. Pop music with a lot of "Ooh, baby, baby" stuff, songs about breaking up with girlfriends, and things like that. Nothing was connecting.

> I can honestly say I'm glad I have my birthmark. It made me who I am today. It's my mark of greatness.

Then I felt the inspiration to connect the music, something I love, to my birthmark, something else I love. I also wanted music that sounded different from the typical pop music you hear on the radio. That's how I started writing inspirational songs, and everything just clicked from there. Sometimes I like writing the whole song. Sometimes I like adjusting the lyrics of songs that are played on the radio.

"Stand Alone" is one of my early favorites. It's actually getting back at the kids who made fun of me. I first heard the original song when I was 8 years old. It was in the animated movie *The Quest for Camelot*, which had a blind character who sang "Stand Alone." Now that I'm older I've added some phrases of my own, phrases that focus more on facial differences.

Despite all the lies I've faced 'em and I've tried
And now my heart knows just what it means to fight
For I've felt all the pain and I've heard your lies
But I have learned how to survive.

With this mark, I've embraced
The kiss the angel put on my face.
I share my world with no one else,
All by myself, I stand alone.

It's the message I want other kids with facial differences to hear. I'm saying, "Hey, I stand alone. I don't care what you say about me or anyone else with facial differences." We don't need society to tell us what we're supposed to look like.

My music has inspired me to take it to the next step and start the Stephen Dale Project. I want to make the world a better place for people living with vascular malformations, birthmarks, cleft palates, scars, or other facial differences. I do that by posting my music on my website along with pictures of famous people who have facial differences. Singer Aaron Neville has a facial birthmark, and Tina Turner has a port wine stain birthmark like I do. NFL quarterback Drew Brees has a birthmark on his right cheek. Anchorman Tom Brokaw and Oscar-nominated actor Joaquin Phoenix were each born with a cleft palate. I want kids to see that the sky is the limit for what they can achieve. I also include links to inspirational movies and plays and links to websites where kids can find help and support.

The response has been amazing. I love going through all the emails, reading the impact I'm having on people's lives. I hear from parents and kids, and I can see that I'm doing this for other people, not just for me. It turns out I don't have to stand alone.

Because of all that, I can honestly say I'm glad I have my birthmark. It made me who I am today. I wouldn't take all the money in the world to have it removed. It's my mark of greatness.

I'm finishing up high school and heading off to college soon. I plan to keep writing music. I want to write that magical song that gets to your core and makes you cry. It's time for the next step—to inspire all sorts of people, even those without facial differences.

Learn more at stephendale.com.

Daryn's Takeaways

· ·

Stephen's story shows the power of the mind. Stephen decided for himself what his birthmark represents. We each have that power to define ourselves.

What is something in your life that others may define as a negative but you can choose to define as a positive?

Raisin Hope

Saul Raisin,
professional cyclist and brain injury survivor

I'm here to tell you that spinning your wheels is a good thing. It has led me to my dream career as a professional cyclist, helped me recover from what doctors called "a sure to be terminal" brain injury, and best of all brought me to the love of my life.

I'm 24 years old and I have dreamed most of my life of wearing the yellow victory jersey in the Tour de France. Doctors would tell you it's amazing that you see me alive at all. But I've been proving doctors and doubters wrong my entire life.

Just about everything great I've accomplished I've done on a bike. I first fell in love with cycling when I was growing up in Dalton, Georgia. I started competing in small town races on my mountain bike and I haven't stopped riding since.

Doctors might tell you I shouldn't be able to ride at all. I was born with severe curvature of the spine. I have 42 percent curvature. This usually causes the chest to be caved in. Instead mine is more of an hourglass shape. That means I actually have increased lung capacity and can take in twice as much air as the normal person.

My lungs, along with my larger-than-normal heart, have served me well as I've gone after my dream of becoming one of the best cyclists in the world. The big dream was to win the Tour de France. Just like Lance Armstrong beat the odds after battling cancer, I intended to beat the odds following a devastating brain injury.

I don't remember anything about the accident, but teammates, friends, and family have helped me fill in the blanks. It happened in April 2006 southwest of Paris. I was competing in a tune-up race for my first grand tour, Tour d'Italia. It was just a training race for my team and me to get some speed in our legs on a flat course.

We were just about a mile and a half from the finish line when some gravel on the road caused me to crash into the gutter. I landed on my head, facedown in the gravel. Even though I was wearing a helmet, my face took the brunt of the impact.

The accident didn't appear that serious at the time. Friends tell me I was responsive and talking. Team officials called my parents back in the United States and told them I had broken my collarbone. This would hardly be alarming news to my folks since I'd broken my collarbone four times before in other accidents.

Just 30 hours later my parents received another call telling them I had slipped into a coma. The hospital needed permission to do emergency surgery. My parents were told to come to France right away, although doctors didn't expect me to live through the night.

When my parents arrived, the doctors talked to them about donating my organs. On the outside chance that I did live, they said my parents should expect me to spend the rest of my life in a wheelchair. That would be the best-case scenario.

My parents lived through this hell for about a week, when one day the team doctor came to get them. He was crying, and my parents feared I had died. "No," he told them, "Saul's awake. You need to come immediately."

My parents tell me that I was hardly alert and sitting up in bed, but I was responsive. The only faint memory I have of this time and the coma was my mom beside the bed singing "Twinkle, Twinkle, Little Star," the same song she had sung to me when I was a little boy. Indeed, Mom says that's what she sang over and over again as she kept vigil by my bed. So if you ever have a loved one who is unconscious, I'm here to tell you that what you say to him or her does get through.

After a month of being alert and stable, I could go back to Georgia. That's when the real work began. I went to the Shepard Center, a rehabilitation hospital in Atlanta specializing in spinal cord injuries and brain injuries like mine.

I had to relearn everything. It's hard to explain the scope. It was like being a baby again; but in addition, I couldn't move my left side. And it was more than just having to learn to walk, talk, read, and write. I had to learn what reading and writing were.

I remember looking at a simple first-grade math book and I couldn't do the equations. That was really hard, realizing how far I had to go to climb back.

My parents also needed training. I had damage to the right temporal lobe of my brain, which is the part that handles social appropriateness. I could be in the middle of a public place and suddenly start talking dirty. My parents had to learn how to help me learn how to integrate back into society.

> The accident didn't appear that serious at the time, but 30 hours later my parents received a call telling them I was in a coma.

One of the strangest things was that I couldn't get it into my injured mind that I had a brain injury. Every single day the therapists would ask me, "Saul, do you know why you're here?" I could never answer them. I thought it might be for my broken collarbone. "No," they explained patiently, "you're here because you have a brain injury." The next day we'd have to go through the whole conversation again.

Finally, one day, they let me check my email. I had something like 1,200 messages waiting for me. People like Lance Armstrong were writing to wish me well; others wrote saying they were praying for me.

I read about 20 of them and was totally confused. "What are they talking about?" I wondered. I was in no pain. I was just extremely tired all the time from all the physical and occupational therapy I had to do all day long.

Still at the computer, I googled my name and suddenly almost 200,000 search results came up. "Oh, I must've gotten a lot of coverage because I won the Tour d'Italia race," I told myself, not having a clue!

But then I started clicking on some of the items. "Saul Raisin Has Emergency Brain Surgery," "Saul Raisin in Coma," the headlines read. That's when I finally understood. I broke down crying because I realized the agony I must have put my family and friends through. I was determined not to let them down.

As I regained my strength, I had the chance to ride a stationary bike in the physical therapy room. That was the first time I thought, "I just might be able to get back to cycling."

I worked my way up over the weeks from the stationary bike to what we call "rollers," which is an actual bike mounted on something that works like a treadmill. This is a real balance test. Mom got on one side and Dad on the other. I had the hang of it right away! I eventually begged my doctors for permission to take my bike out on the road.

They gave me the green light but only if I rode uphill and only if my parents followed me in the car. That first ride on the road was the best of my entire life. I just rode and rode and rode.

The early days with all the riding were exhilarating but also concerning to the doctors. It appeared the "fatigue factor" part of my brain wasn't working. I wasn't getting the signal that my body was spent. This could be dangerous as I could literally exercise myself to death or at least injure myself. I've now been able to get that sensation back. Trust me, when I go out for a huge training ride, now I feel it.

I slowly but surely improved my condition and felt ready to make some appearances at familiar cycling events. One of the early ones was Tour de California, an eight-day, 700-mile race across the state. I rode every stage before the races as a "Raisin Hope" event. There had been so much coverage of my challenges in the racing community that people were excited to see me back on the bike.

After the event I was at Los Angeles International Airport waiting to fly home to Georgia. While I was waiting for my flight, I was speaking French with a woman I met from Luxembourg. One of the strange side effects of the brain injury is that I now speak better French than before the accident. Doctors can't explain that one, but there's no question I'm better at the language I was trying to pick up in my many training trips to France.

As I was finishing that conversation, I turned around and saw another woman with the most beautiful blue eyes I had ever seen. "You're Saul Raisin," she gasped.

"Yes, I am," I confirmed.

"I've been praying for you," she said.

That might seem like a very strange thing for a stranger to tell me. I quickly found out she was Aleeza Zabriskie. Her brother, David, is a professional cyclist. Because of that she, like many in the cycling world, had been following my story.

What happened from there makes my life like a movie. Aleeza and I talked for five or six minutes before we had to get on our respective planes. She was flying to her hometown of Salt Lake City. I couldn't stop thinking about her all the way home to Atlanta.

I started to text message her as soon as my plane landed, only to find she had emailed me as soon as she got in. I don't know if I believed in love at first sight before, but I do now. Aleeza is truly the girl of my dreams. I soon moved out to Utah to be with her. We were married in December and have now moved together to France.

With the start of the 2008 racing season, I planned on returning to train with my team Credit Agricole. My goal was nothing short of winning the Tour de France.

Unfortunately I fought my way back from the accident and brain injury only to have my dream of being a professional cyclist taken away. In November 2007, right before my wedding and just before rejoining the team, I received word that the French doctors would not release me to race. I fought back the tears as I heard the news. Although I did very well on all my neuro-psych tests, the doctors said it would be too dangerous if I were to crash and hit my head again.

> With the love and support of my teammates, friends, and family, including my new wife, there are no limits to how far I can go.

It was difficult to take in that 13 years of hard training were over, along with my dream. I've always said that if you do your best in anything, you can be happy and content knowing you gave it your best shot. I will always stand by this motto, even as I find myself having to redefine my dreams. I did my all to get back to the sport I love. I will never have to ask "What if?"

Of course, there are still challenges. I do have to ask "What's next?" Part of the answer lies with the more than five million Americans who live with a brain injury each year. I want to grow my Raisin Hope Fund into a foundation to help them. I've shown people to never give up and always fight to the finish. With the love and support of my teammates, friends, and family, including my new wife, I believe there are no limits to how far I can go.

Together we are Raisin Hope.

To learn more about Saul, visit saulraisin.com.

Daryn's Takeaways

When I first interviewed Saul, his dream of returning to professional cycling was still very much alive. Just as this book was going to print, he received the disappointing news that doctors wouldn't clear him to rejoin his old team. Everyone who knows and cheers for Saul was crushed.

Meanwhile, Saul simply found another opportunity to inspire and show "What's Possible!" It's more than possible that all our original dreams won't come true. It's possible that even when you give your all and then some, factors outside your control will bring those dreams to an end.

But Saul shows me that it comes down to always getting back on the proverbial bike. He got back on after the crash. He's getting back on now that his dream has been denied. This time the road will take him in a direction he can't imagine today. That can be scary. But in his heart Saul knows and shows that he won't get to those new dreams and adventures if he doesn't take the first step of simply getting back on the bike.

Have you had a big dream fall through and chosen to stay in the disappointment rather than getting back on your own bike? What might be possible if you dared to take another ride?

Part 2

· ·

Survivor Stories: Claiming Health and Healing

Feel Your Boobies®

Leigh Hurst,
breast cancer survivor and creator of
Feel Your Boobies Foundation

That's right, I want you to "feel your boobies."

I'll bet I got your attention with that phrase, and that's exactly what I want to do. I want you to feel your boobies because I want you to save your life just as I saved mine.

In 2001 I was the last woman in the world who expected to get breast cancer. The thought never even crossed my mind. I was in my early thirties living in New York City and working as a business consultant. I worked hard, traveled a lot for my job, and played hard. I was in great shape and I have no history of breast cancer in my family.

Sure, I heard the warnings and advice that women should do breast self-exams. I just never thought about it. Those mint-green brochures we all see in our doctors' offices seemed so clinical. I honestly didn't pay attention.

But in the normal, everyday activities of showering, getting dressed, and so on, I did have my hands on my breasts and I was aware of what was normal for my body. That awareness saved my life.

Somewhere around the time I was 31, I started noticing an area in one of my breasts that felt hard and different. I didn't really pay attention though since I couldn't actually describe it as a lump.

But then more changes came and I became a little more nervous. I did what we women do and asked my girlfriends, "Hey, does this ever happen to you?" When my girlfriends assured me that their bodies were not acting the same way, I grew more concerned.

Apparently I was alone in my concern because I showed the worrisome area to doctors on three different occasions, and each one told me it was nothing to worry about. First I would let the doctor do her normal breast exam. If she didn't feel it, I figured it was no big deal. Then I would take her hand and put it on the area so she could feel what I was talking about. Still, each one said, "I don't think it's anything to worry about."

> I heard the warnings to do breast self-exams, but I just never thought about it.

A couple of years later I moved back to the small town in central Pennsylvania where I grew up. I was at a new doctor's office for my annual checkup, and just to make my chart complete I mentioned the area to the nurse practitioner. "I've been watching this area," I told her. "Well, y'know, it can't hurt to get that checked out," she said. She wrote me a prescription to get a diagnostic mammogram. I needed that because I was way too young to start getting mammograms.

I didn't think much about the mammogram appointment, which was unfortunate because it turned out to be a really bad day. Normally my mom would go to something like that with me. But my parents were out of town on vacation, so I went by myself, having no idea what to expect.

The technicians did their job. I now know they usually only do two films of each breast, but that day they did about eight films on the side that had the lump. Finally I asked, "Is this normal? Or are you guys just looking around?"

"Well," they admitted, "this area looks suspicious." They showed me the little specks that appeared on the film. "These types of things can be problematic or they might just be calcifications. We're just trying to get a closer look. We want to do an ultrasound right now."

That's when I started to get really scared. The ultrasound came back to show that what I had was more a mass than a cyst. I remember the nurse holding my hand and asking, "Is there anyone at home for you to talk to?"

I felt so alone. All I could think was "I'm single. I've moved back to this small town. I'm 33 years old and I want my mommy."

Three weeks later they did a biopsy. The next day the surgeon called me and said, "I'm shocked to say that this is actually cancer. It appears to be the type that has an 85 to 95 percent survival rate." When I heard the phrase "survival rate," I thought, "I cannot even wrap my head around what she's saying here."

The diagnosis ended up being Stage 1 breast cancer, and the doctors suggested a lumpectomy, in which they just take part of the breast and check out the lymph nodes. The surgery went well, but because of my age and because my tumor was actually twice as big as doctors had expected, they also recommended that I take chemotherapy. So I had the full experience: surgery, chemo, and radiation.

I actually felt pretty good physically while I was going through chemo, and I was able to exercise on a regular basis. I started telling some of my girlfriends with whom I worked out, "Y'know, you guys have to feel your boobies."

We laughed about the phrase, but my point was that if breast cancer could happen to me, it could happen to anyone, and it's important for all women to know their bodies and be aware of any changes.

My friends and I were joking around about the phrase "Feel Your Boobies" and how it would make a fun T-shirt. Then one of my friends who is an art teacher said, "If you're serious about that, I would love to help you design a logo. My aunts had breast cancer, and I would love a way to give back."

Together we came up with the original Feel Your Boobies logo and had a lot of fun looking at different T-shirts it could go on. I ordered about 100 shirts and thought that would be it. Little did I know my inspiration was about to take off.

Another group of friends back in New York wanted to do a two-day breast cancer walk with me to celebrate the end of my treatment. It was the two-day Avon Walk in New York City. We decided to call ourselves the Feel Your Boobies team.

I brought the extra T-shirts with me just in case anyone was interested. I also printed some business cards on my computer.

The first morning of the walk I had about 30 T-shirts in my backpack. I sold all of them in less than an hour. The rest of my inventory sold out the next morning when excited women demanded to meet me first thing so they, too, could buy a Feel Your Boobies T-shirt.

All my friends and I were thinking, "What the heck is going on here?" That was the first time I realized what a good idea this was. People were responding to the phrase for the same reason I felt the need to say it. They liked the fresh, feel-good attitude. It's not sad and morbid. It's fun!

So Feel Your Boobies was born. It actually started as a company, but I came to realize it is so much more. As a company, we would just be a T-shirt operation, but as a nonprofit organization, we are a message about awareness. The T-shirt is just one of many vehicles our organization uses to convey the message.

We are promoting the healthy, proactive habit of being breast- and body-aware. I just think it is so important to do that with humor and empowerment rather than with fear and clinical lessons about the "right way" to do a breast self-exam. We give some specific tips on our website, but bottom line, ladies, I really just want you to put your hands on your boobs and get to know what feels normal and what doesn't.

I now run the Feel Your Boobies Foundation out of my garage, which I've painted pink. Gone is that lost and lonely feeling I had the day of my mammogram. I feel like I've found my purpose. It's just incredible to have a young woman in her twenties tell me she had a lump checked out because she saw a Feel Your Boobies sign somewhere. "It made me laugh," she said. "I checked myself that night in the shower. The lump was concerning enough to get it removed. I would never have paid attention if I first hadn't chuckled at that Feel Your Boobies car magnet that I saw."

Moments like that make me feel so lucky for this whole breast cancer experience.

Yes, lucky. The life lessons that I learned were things I was already trying to work on. I made the decision to leave New York City for the slower pace of my small town because I didn't think the stressed-out, fast-paced life was what I was about anymore.

Surviving breast cancer has helped me get even clearer about protecting my time and saying "No." Upon returning to my job, if I was asked to make a last-minute trip across the country, I felt confident in saying, "No, I'm not going to be able to make the meeting in person, but I'd be happy to be available by conference call." I was willing to be replaced if it came down to it, but it never did. My experience with cancer gave me the strength I needed to be able to say, "I'm making decisions for my own well-being and I'm going to do as much as I feel is fair and reasonable. Beyond that, I'm putting my foot down."

For people who are currently facing a tough time physically or otherwise, I think you have to be open to the possibility that what is happening in your life right now might not make sense. But being self-aware can help you turn it into something good.

That certainly is how it worked out for me. I didn't expect breast cancer and I wouldn't have picked it, but the health challenge has helped me create the life I want. And it has brought me a sense of purpose that I knew was lacking in my old life.

So I would say be open to what is possible and, of course, don't forget to Feel Your Boobies!

You can learn more at FeelYourBoobies.com.

Daryn's Takeaways

I love how Leigh acknowledges that during hard times the stuff that happens to us might not seem to make sense. How many times has each of us asked ourselves, "Why is this happening to me?"

I think Leigh nails it when she talks about being open to the possibility that whatever you're going through might lead to something better. That way of thinking gives you permission to dislike your current circumstances, but it also leaves you open to hope and to the idea that something bigger than you could even dream for yourself just might be around the corner.

What circumstance in your life right now don't you like? Can you be open to the idea it is actually leading you to a better situation?

Beauty from the Bad

Ramy Gafni,
makeup artist, entrepreneur, and cancer survivor

You know those people who are thankful for getting cancer because they say they needed a wake-up call to live life the right way? I wasn't one of them. Even before I was diagnosed with lymphoma at the age of 31, I was a really nice person. I was kind to children and animals and did good in the world. I didn't even take things for granted. So cancer wasn't my wake-up call. But it was my chance to put beauty in the world, something I was determined to do because it was the one thing I could control.

I'm in love with the art of transformation. I love to see how simple makeup application or an eyebrow shaping can transform a woman's face in minutes. I don't care if it happens on one of the many celebrities I've worked for or my everyday clients. The process is magic every time.

In 1995 I was living my dream, working as the makeup director in a major New York City salon. After years of school and paying my dues at a department store makeup counter, this was my chance to put my name on the map. I was doing makeup, getting a lot of press for fabulous eyebrow styling, and developing a makeup line for the salon.

With all that hard work, it didn't surprise me that I seemed to be tired all the time. At one point it seemed everyone at the salon was coming down with the flu. That's when I noticed I was having some trouble breathing. When I inhaled deeply I would feel a sharp pain from my lung through my shoulder. I figured I just needed antibiotics, so I found a doctor near my house and went for what I thought would be a quick fix.

I honestly was not concerned when he ran a few tests. My white blood cell count came back a bit high. I figured no big deal. He ordered X-rays, which showed something cloudy around my chest. I figured the X-ray technician had messed it up because he was on his cell phone the whole time.

By the time I was referred to the oncologist, things were starting to look more serious. When the doctor informed me I had lymphoma, the news hit me like a ton of bricks.

I went through five months of chemotherapy. I lost all my hair, and because I was on steroids I gained a lot of weight. But I only took one sick day in that entire five months. My regular clients were amazing. Instead of freaking out about my appearance, they were loyal and encouraging and kept coming back.

I wish I could say the same about the salon management. They did everything they could to make me uncomfortable and to force me to quit. For instance, as makeup director, my job had always included hiring new makeup staff. One day in the middle of my chemo, they suddenly hired a new makeup artist without consulting me. When I complained, their response was, "So what are you going to do about it?"

Remember how I told you I was already a good person? Part of that was always choosing to take the high road. The high road takes you to good places, and the low road takes you to bad places. So I kept on going, just focusing on my recovery and seeing my regular clients.

Then I discovered the salon management was funneling my clients to the new makeup artist. A customer with an appointment to see me would show up and ask for me. She was told I wasn't in today, but this other makeup artist would love to see her. One of my clients was so concerned after her appointment that she called to see if I was OK and why I wasn't at work that day.

When I assured her that I was indeed at work, I put two and two together and again confronted management. Their response again was, "So what are you going to do about it?"

"Well, I'll tell you this," I informed them, "I'm not going to quit. First of all, I'm not a quitter, and second of all, I need my health insurance."

"Fine, then," the boss said. "If you're not going to quit, we're going to have to let you go. You're just not the pretty boy we hired." Honest to God, that's what he said.

I packed up my things and moved my business into my tiny Manhattan apartment. As I did, two wonderful things happened.

First let me tell you about my book. The inspiration came during those months of chemotherapy. I would look at the other patients and wish I could teach all of them some of the simple beauty tricks I knew. What can you do when you lose your hair, including your eyebrows and eyelashes? What can you do when your skin turns an odd yellow color during chemo or your cheeks become extra red during radiation? I knew what to do because it was all happening to me.

> I couldn't control the cancer, the treatment, the hair loss, the weight gain...but I could control putting good in the world.

The book started as a collection of good beauty rituals and evolved into a bit of a spiritual guide about how to celebrate your own inner beauty. It took eight years to get that book published, but if I do nothing else with my life, I know I've made a wonderful contribution to the world.

I take the book with me when I speak to groups of cancer patients. I usually begin by walking into a room of women going through cancer care. Their arms are crossed, and they have doubt written across their foreheads, as if to say, "Screw you, buddy. I've got cancer. What are you going to tell me, that 'Pink is my color'?"

The first thing I do is show them pictures of me going through treatment. Big, bald, and bloated. "This was me," I tell them. That's when they literally sit up and think, "Maybe this guy has something to say."

Then I call one of them up and do a one-minute makeup job. This is what my style is all about: minimum makeup, maximum impact. I like a woman to look natural, not as if she is wearing a birthday cake on her face. When the cancer patients see I can make that happen in about one minute, I've won them over and I share my secrets.

The business side of my life continued to be challenging. No sooner had I been fired from the salon when another salon called me. I was told they were hiring and I should come over to talk about becoming their makeup director. That meeting was like an online date gone bad since I was still in the middle of chemo. "Oh, you don't look like your picture," they said.

I explained what I was going through and assured them I was working through it and would be on the other side of all this within a few months. I was shocked when they now said, "We're actually not hiring right now." This was despite the fact they had practically given me the job on the phone.

These developments meant that my apartment became Ramy Makeup Central. My clients were wonderful about coming there. I would shape their eyebrows and recommend makeup from various stores.

Some clients suggested I sell all these products out of my apartment. I had a bigger idea. I wanted my own makeup line. This had always been a dream of mine. I had done research for the salon to start a makeup line for it but was fired before I could do this.

I knew how. And I knew where. But I didn't have the cash. Still big and bald from the chemo, I went to a manufacturing facility in Toronto. The business was run by a couple who understandably wanted to know how much money I had to spend on things like research and development.

Honestly, if you took every single cent I had—savings, possessions, pocket change—it might have added up to $15,000. The scale of the project I was asking for needed a budget of about $500,000! Clearly I was out of my league.

I refused to take no for an answer though. I came back day after day. I simply refused to leave. I shared with them my entire story. I told them, "I'm publishing a book, magazines are writing about me, and if you give me this shot, one day I will be your biggest customer."

As it turns out, the husband was also a cancer survivor! He had had tumors all over his body, and it was a miracle he survived. My story must have touched him because he finally said, "Oh, all right."

That amazing couple disregarded the minimum order and waived the research and development fee. For about $12,000 I had five lipstick shades, one blush, two eyeshadows, one eyeliner, mascara, three foundation concealer sticks, and my signature Miracle Brow compact.

Things snowballed from there. Just selling from my apartment, I sold out in about three months. Within a year I had my products in Bergdorf Goodman, one of the most prestigious department stores in New York. I'm now also selling on QVC, in boutiques and salons across the country, and of course on Ramy.com.

My best news of all is that I've reached 10 years of remission, which, according to the doctors, means I am cured of the lymphoma.

I look back on that one very bad year and shake my head. As I said before, I would never have asked for any of it. But I feel empowered because I made the choice to make beauty out of all the bad. I learned it's all about controlling what you can. I couldn't control the cancer, the treatment, the hair loss, the weight gain, or even losing my job. But I could control putting good in the world. Between the book and the speaking appearances, so many people have benefited. That is a beautiful thing indeed.

For more on Ramy's makeup go to ramybeautytherapy.com or ramy.com.

Ramy Gafni's *Cancer Beauty Therapy: The Ultimate Guide to Looking and Feeling Great While Living with Cancer* **was published by M. Evans & Co., September 2005.**

Daryn's Takeaways

First of all, I love Ramy's honesty and humor. He didn't need cancer to teach him to be a better person. He already was a good person! Yet instead of getting stuck in "Why me?" he moved on, choosing to control what he could.

We all are capable of falling into the trap of focusing on circumstances we cannot change. Where in your own life can you see an opportunity, as did Ramy, to create beauty from the bad?

Dead and Alive

Megan Kelley Hall,
survivor of cancer and heart surgery, writer

In April 2006 I died for 96 minutes. Not in the "I saw a tunnel of light" or even "Get out the paddles and bring her back" sense. But at age 32 I suffered a series of strokes, one causing partial vision loss, and I ended up having to undergo open-heart surgery. Yet surprisingly it was the best thing that could have ever happened for my career—and quite possibly my life.

So how does a seemingly healthy 32-year-old go from walking on the beach to undergoing major open-heart surgery? Well, this is my story. If it seems hard to believe, imagine going through it yourself.

I'm not vain, but I've never liked my scars. I was a cancer survivor at age 2 and was deemed cancer-free after 18 months of chemotherapy and radiation. The only evidence of that experience was a large radiation scar on my back, which I had removed in my teens. This left me with scars that crisscrossed my back—something I could keep hidden from the world.

Now it's ironic that I have a foot-long scar stretching from my neck to my midsection. At first I couldn't look at it. It's red and raised and very noticeable. Often I'll catch someone looking at my scar when it's exposed. But it doesn't bother me now. It's proof that I'm here, that I survived. This is something I can't hide. And I won't, because I am a survivor.

My health issues started unexpectedly with what I thought was a migraine. The vision loss was a transient ischemic attack (TIA), where bits of calcium or cholesterol were flicking off my carotid arteries and shooting into my eyes and my brain. It could have easily caused a debilitating stroke. My doctors considered it lucky that I only lost partial vision.

I was a medical enigma. No one knew why or how I was having these attacks. I had low cholesterol. My EKGs, CT scans, MRIs, MRAs, and echocardiograms were normal. I'd had no ramifications from my childhood cancer. Where was this all coming from? Why me and why now? After months of testing they said it was a fluke and would probably never happen again.

Until it did.

After another major attack during a simple walk on the beach, my doctor scheduled me for a carotid artery angiogram (and possible angioplasty). In that bright, cold operating room where I was surrounded by computer monitors, video screens, and a cardiovascular and neurology team, I had my first major panic attack. They couldn't sedate me because they needed me alert in case of a stroke. They questioned me the entire time: What is your name? Who is the president? What is the date? What is your daughter's name? I broke down, picturing my then 3-year-old waiting outside with my husband, wondering what was wrong with her mommy.

> Second chances are rare. If you're lucky enough to be given one, make the most of it. It's up to you to create the life you want.

The radiation treatment I received as a baby had aged my carotid arteries. They called it radiation-accelerated atherosclerosis. The carotid stenting was a success, but for the next year I never stopped worrying. Would the stent work? What was that flicker in my vision? I took a never-ending supply of blood thinners, antidepressants, antianxiety and cholesterol-lowering pills, iron supplements—pills to calm me down and pills to perk me up. My medicine cabinet looked as if it should belong to a rock star, not a 32-year-old mother of a toddler who rarely even indulged in a glass of wine.

After seeking therapy for a year to stop my panic attacks, I had another TIA. The stent wasn't working, and major surgery was my only option. On April 13, 2006, I had a 9½-hour open-heart surgery. My body temperature was dropped to well below 90°F, my heart stopped, all brain activity quieted, and I was put on a heart-lung machine. The machine was turned off during the riskiest part of the procedure. The longer I stayed in that limbo state between life and death, the higher the risk of getting me back to the proper mental state—or of bringing me back at all. Luckily the procedure was skillfully conducted by the chief of cardiac surgery at Brigham and Women's Hospital in Boston. When I became fully conscious two days later in the ICU, I was aching all over, having been sliced open from the side of my neck down to the bottom of my rib cage.

My anesthesiologist told me (after the fact, thankfully) that they packed my head in ice and lowered my body temperature and put me on the heart-lung machine. Then, amazingly, they took me off the heart-lung machine for 96 minutes—*96 minutes!* I jokingly said, "Oh, so you flatlined me." I had images of Julia Roberts and Kiefer Sutherland jolting each other back to life. He deadpanned, "Basically you were as close to death as humanly possible without actually dying."

It wasn't exactly smooth sailing after that. I underwent another heart surgery after a blood clot in my arm alerted them to the liter of fluid surrounding my heart. Then my left lung, surrounded by fluid, shriveled down to one-fifth the size of my right lung. Another day, another operation. The procedure was successful, and I was discharged from the hospital—permanently.

Today I'm left with my Frankenstein scar and my sternum held together with little twist ties. I knew they wrapped my sternum in titanium wire and I imagined a large coil wrapped top to bottom. During my postsurgery X-ray I was shocked to discover seven little twist ties with the ends poking out. I joked with my doctor, "Which brand of twist tie did you use, Glad or Hefty?"

When I finally got home, I couldn't lift anything over 10 pounds, couldn't drive, and could barely care for myself, let alone take care of my daughter. My parents' house became day care. An entire summer without cleaning, driving, or working may seem enjoyable, but I spent most of the time counting down the hours (even minutes) until I could take pain medication.

Being couch- or bedridden for months gave me plenty of time to reflect on my life. I realized that the premature birth of my daughter—born 12 weeks early and weighing only 2½ pounds—was most likely a blessing in disguise. Piper is now a very healthy and happy 5-year-old. Yet if I had carried her to term, the risk of my having a major heart attack or debilitating stroke was incredibly high. At that time I had no idea about the damaged state of my carotids. The added pressure of pregnancy could have been disastrous, even deadly.

It was during that period that I also realized that my dreams of being a published author had never been fulfilled. Yes, I'd had articles published in a few national magazines and had started a fledgling literary publicity company, but my dream of getting an agent and walking into a bookstore to pick up a copy of my own book was just that—a dream.

Up until that point my life stretched out before me, limitless. I had all the time in the world to become a "real" writer. But my outlook changed. Every time I saw the foot-long red gash on my chest, I was reminded of my mortality. I knew that nobody lived forever, but I'd never hovered over that thin line between life and death before. All the clichés about life became astoundingly true. Life isn't a dress rehearsal. You only live once. Life is what happens when you're making other plans.

So my plan was to write—for real. I took out the manuscript I'd been toying with for years and worked on it with a passion I'd never had before. I feverishly contacted agents and editors, and within a few months I landed an agent at one of the top literary agencies in New York. Not only did she love my novel, but she read my blog that chronicled my medical experiences and it made her laugh out loud. I used my blog as a way of funneling my frustrations and anxieties about my surgeries and infused it with a good dose of humor, which frankly was the only way to get through that crazy time. After several months of edits and rewrites and rejections and all of the things associated with getting your first book sold, the unimaginable happened. I received a two-book deal with a major publisher.

By May 2007 I also had an article in *Glamour* magazine and our fledgling book publicity company was getting praise, recognition, and *New York Times* best-selling authors as clients. The dream was becoming a reality.

Now when people ask me if I have a whole new outlook and appreciation of life, I often surprise them by saying "no." I've never been a "glass half full" kind of girl. I don't feel particularly blessed, and I don't believe that I've been given this chance to do something profoundly important. But I now realize that life is short and unpredictable. What we do with our lives is completely up to us, but it's important to know that second chances are rare. And if you're lucky enough to be given one, make the most of it. I don't advocate living like there's no tomorrow because that can be construed as living recklessly. It's up to you to create the life you want. Enjoy those around you. Love what you do. Be the person you want to be. Never take anything for granted. It sounds easy enough, but how many people actually live that way?

Learn more at megankelleyhall.com.

One Step at a Time

Kelly Perkins,
heart transplant recipient and mountain climber

I climb some of the best-known peaks in the world.
And when I do, I bring along climbing gear, food supplies, and the heart
of a woman I never met beating inside my chest.

I'm the last person who ever expected to need a heart transplant.
In the early 1990s I was living a dream life, married to my college
sweetheart, Craig. We both had thriving careers in real estate and shared
our passion for the outdoors.

I admit it. I was a bit of a health nut. My friends called me "Temple
Kelly" because I was so conscientious about what I ate and how I
exercised. It was very much a lifestyle for me.

So were the mountains. I grew up in Lake Tahoe, California, where the
mountains were practically part of my DNA. From the moment we met,
Craig and I loved to spend all of our free time hiking, backpacking, and
climbing. We celebrated our fifth wedding anniversary by backpacking
across Europe, hiking mountains in Italy and Switzerland.

It was when we got back from that trip that I noticed something wasn't
right. I felt rapid heartbeats when I was just sitting still or lying in bed at
night. I didn't know if something was wrong, but I knew something about
my heart was different.

I went to my general practitioner to get checked out and he practically laughed me out of his office. To be fair, I know I did look the picture of a perfectly fit and healthy 30-year-old woman at that visit. My resting heart rate was only 50 beats per minute. Still I felt like something was wrong. The doctor gave me a card for a local psychiatrist and sent me on my way.

About a month later Craig and I had plans to head up to the mountains for a long weekend with friends. I knew we would be away from phones and any kind of medical care. My gut told me I needed to go back and have the doctor check just one more time.

I risked having this doctor think I was cuckoo and begged him to do one more EKG. This time my resting heart rate was 200 beats per minute! That's four times its normal pace.

Now the doctor was frightened. I was frightened. It was my last moment of normality because from that point on, my life became one giant medical crisis.

The doctor immediately admitted me to the local hospital where the head cardiologist informed me, "We have a serious problem here."

At this point I still thought, "I'm the healthiest person I know. They'll just give me some kind of pill and I'll be on my way." I even thought there was still a chance Craig and I could make the weekend backpacking trip with our friends. They airlifted me to another Southern California hospital about an hour away.

The heart biopsy spelled out a much different story. It showed there was scarring on the surface of my heart, probably caused by a virus that I never realized I'd had. By the time I was in the hospital and doctors were able to look at my heart, the virus was gone; the damage was done. The doctors focused on trying to put out this fire and get me back to normal. The plan was to hold on long enough for my heart to recover on its own. Instead I started a three-year medical and emotional odyssey.

That scarring caused my heart to constantly be erratic. For no reason it would start racing on its own. I had to take a cocktail of drugs, sometimes as many as 28 pills a day. It was no lifestyle at all.

My condition only got worse. Finally after three years I went into congestive heart failure, which meant my other organs were now being compromised because they weren't getting the blood and oxygen they needed. When that happens, things go downhill pretty quickly. The doctors were out of options. They told my family, "She needs a heart transplant."

I was actually very lucky. Some people wait for months and years with no heart ever becoming available. In my case, within 24 hours of my going on the list, a heart became available for me.

I learned a little about the donor at the time of transplant. She was 40 years old, from back East. She had been visiting Southern California, where she had a horseback riding accident and died in the hospital.

It was such a strange physical sensation to wake up from the operation. I had lived so long with an ever-weakening heart. Now I had this robust pump pushing fluid through my skinny little veins and arteries. I felt like I was full of too much pressure and I was going to burst any moment. That experience took feeling bloated to a new level. I looked down and saw this scar that seemed way too delicate and insecure for the powerful heart now beating inside me.

> The heart biopsy showed scarring on the surface of my heart, probably caused by a virus.

I was 90 pounds when I left the hospital with the new heart. I immediately went to work setting new goals for getting strong again. It wasn't too long before I knew what I really wanted to do: get back to the mountains. That would represent reclaiming the old Kelly.

My wonderful husband was with me all the way. When I was first diagnosed, I was terrified because I had taken him away from the life that I knew he wanted. But from day one he insisted this didn't just happen to me; it happened to both of us. We were a team. I know I couldn't have made it through this without Craig.

Half Dome in Yosemite National Park was the first mountain I wanted to climb. It's a round mountain that has been cut in half by the forces of nature. I could identify with the symbolism. Even though it was broken, it still stood as tall as the surrounding peaks. Ten months after receiving my new heart, I made it to Half Dome's summit.

That first climb set the tone for all the climbs to follow. Each peak Craig and I conquer has purpose and meaning. We climbed Mount Aspiring in New Zealand to bring attention to organ donation in a country with some of the lowest organ donation rates in the world. We climbed Mount Kilimanjaro, the tallest peak on the continent of Africa, to commemorate medical milestones that have been achieved since the first heart transplant ever, which took place in South Africa in 1967.

Then and now, my new heart works at about 70 percent of what's normal for the average female my age and size. But despite the need to progress more slowly, the effort is worth it. As it says in a favorite poem, I focus on the step, not the stumble. Somehow my mind, body, and spirit all come together beautifully to propel me to the top of each mountain.

The most emotional climb had to be Mount Fuji in 1998. We planned this mission to bring attention to a new law in Japan making it easier for families to donate the organs of loved ones. It turned out a very special loved one would be joining our trek.

By this time I had started receiving publicity about my climbs. One Associated Press article was picked up by newspapers across the country. Back on the East Coast, one young woman read the article and started putting pieces of information together. Craig heard the message on our answering machine. "I hope this is the right Kelly Perkins," she said. "I think you have my mother's heart." It was indeed my donor's daughter.

Craig spoke with her and then shared the call with me. He knew this would be very emotional information for me to take in. Heart donations are complicated things. They aren't like receiving a kidney or a liver where your donor can still be alive. The fact that I was living meant a 40-year-old woman had lost her life. Because of that emotional burden, I had chosen up to this point to think of this thing beating in my chest as a pump rather than a heart. Yet here was this woman's daughter, and she had a very unusual request.

When the young woman learned of our next trek up Mount Fuji, she asked that we bring along her mother's ashes and scatter them at the top. Of course, we couldn't refuse. We would do anything for this family.

Craig is the one who knew of the request and carried the donor's ashes up Mount Fuji. He didn't want me to feel pressured to complete the climb if I was having complications on the way up. When we made it to the summit, he presented me with the ashes and a letter from the donor's daughter.

Holding the ashes of the body that once held the heart beating inside me was incredibly emotional and daunting. But it also brought a sense of freedom and belonging, as if the donor family was telling me I have permission now to own this heart. It told me they're happy with where the heart is.

Now before each climb, we notify the family and talk with them. The donor's daughter feels that her mom is going up those mountains too. At the same time, I feel the heart is truly mine.

In so many ways this is not the life my husband and I planned for ourselves. For instance, we always thought we would have children, and now we can't because of my condition. That could be a huge setback, but we've turned it around. We couldn't do all the work we do toward organ donation if we were focused on raising kids. We simply choose to focus on the positive of what's possible.

I am thankful for this entire experience. Because of it I live a less trivial life than I otherwise would have. I have appreciation for the extra time I've been given. My purpose now is to give hope to people who are in a dire physical situation or who are desperate in any way. I want them to see that there are wonderful gifts right around the corner. Perhaps different gifts from what they imagined but wonderful gifts nonetheless. They just need to stay focused on the step, not the stumble.

Read more of Kelly's story in *The Climb of My Life: Scaling Mountains with a Borrowed Heart* **published by Rowan & Littlefield, November 2007.**

> I am thankful for this entire experience. Because of it I live a less trivial life than I otherwise would have.

Champion Teammates

Steve Rom,
cancer survivor and sportswriter

This is the story of the two most unlikely friends you'll ever find. I'm an average-looking, white, Jewish sportswriter. My best friend, Rod Payne, is a 6 foot 4-inch, 300-pound, black Super Bowl champion. This is a story of how we helped each other find new leases on life.

Rod and I met in 2001 in Ann Arbor, Michigan. I was a year or so out of college, starting my sportswriting career. Rod had just finished winning the Super Bowl with the Baltimore Ravens and was fresh into his retirement. More than a dozen surgeries meant his body was done with football.

I met him one day while hanging out at the University of Michigan athletic department. I thought, "This would be a great guy to do a story on." Rod had been an MVP while playing at the University of Michigan, he'd reached the pinnacle of the NFL, and now he was adjusting to life after football. He was coming down off the high of his fabulous career, looking for a new purpose. Meanwhile, I was just getting geared up for mine.

Like with most people I'd written stories about, I figured we'd hang out for a while, I'd write the piece, and then we'd both move on. I wrote that it looked like Rod had found his new calling in broadcasting since he'd just started a new gig at the local sports talk radio station.

Once the story ran in the newspaper, though, Rod and I continued to hang out with each other. We sure did look like an odd pair, as mismatched as Arnold Schwarzenegger and Danny DeVito in the movie *Twins*. We were a funny sight, but we found we had an important experience in common: We were both only children of single mothers. Neither one of us had fathers in our lives when we were growing up.

Somewhere along the way Rod had developed a strength and confidence about himself. Maybe it was his physical presence or his football success, or maybe he was born with it. I, on the other hand, had always been more insecure. I was definitely a loner. It seemed like most people in my life never stuck around, and I figured I had to get through any hard times on my own.

> Somewhere along the way Rod had developed a strength and confidence about himself. I had always been more insecure.

The second half of 2001 was great: I was pursuing the career I loved, I had a wonderful girlfriend, and I enjoyed spending time with my buddy, Rod.

About five months after we met, I went home to Los Angeles to visit my mother as I did every December.

About a week into my trip, I became really sick. I thought it was a severe case of the flu. When I wasn't getting any better, my mom took me to the emergency room at UCLA.

Before I knew it the doctor was standing by my bed telling me I had leukemia—lymphocytic leukemia, whatever that was. Basically I had too many red blood cells and not enough healthy white blood cells. I had to start chemotherapy immediately.

This was like a bad dream. What happened to my great life? I called my boss at the newspaper and told him not to expect me back at work right away. I called my girlfriend. Then I called Rod.

I was supposed to arrive back in Michigan the next day, and Rod was planning to pick me up from the airport.

"Don't pick me up tomorrow," I told him with a very bitter and angry tone in my voice.

He wanted to know why.

"You're not going to believe this," I said. "I have leukemia."

That is honestly all I remember from the conversation. That time was a fog of intense chemo and morphine.

It seems like I went from hanging up the phone to waking up the next day seeing Rod walk into my hospital room. He must have taken one of the first flights out from Michigan.

He looked larger than life. I saw him drop his familiar NFL duffel bag on the white tile floor.

"Hi, Bro," he said. "You ready to knock this out? Let's do this."

It was like a dream—as if Rod were all suited up at the base of the tunnel at the University of Michigan stadium, ready for battle. Only this time I was his teammate and leukemia was the opponent.

I did a complete 180 as far as my mental outlook. I went from bitter to fired up. Here was this Super Bowl champion trying to build a new life. He had his hosting job at the sports talk radio station, but when he heard his buddy was in trouble, he dropped everything and came. We call it OTD—he was "out the door."

People now ask him why he dropped everything and came to my side. He says two things. One, he was trained to go to the call. He was trained to be there for his teammate. And two, he could empathize. With 12 surgeries on his battered body, he knew what it was like to feel down and out in a hospital.

From there Rod set up a game plan, a physical one and a mental one. The physical one meant doing whatever needed to be done to get me going, such as wheeling my IV pole to the bathroom. He corrected the doctors when he thought they weren't paying me enough attention.

Mentally, he made me see that the best way to face this problem was not to be upset and bitter. He made me see that I couldn't go into the game without my head on straight.

He stayed by my bedside until he absolutely had to go back to Michigan. Even then he was on the phone with daily pep talks.

Two months later I was in remission but still facing a bone marrow transplant. This was another low point because I had lost 40 pounds and was getting very frustrated waiting for a bone marrow donor match.

Rod came out again. This time he was determined to whip me into physical shape. He fixed me food and made me eat it, ordering me around like a drill sergeant.

"This is recovery now!" he'd bark. "You think I wanted to eat after all my surgeries?" Then he'd slap down a huge bowl on the table. "This is stew. Eat it!"

And he read me the riot act about getting in better physical shape. "Obviously you're not going to the gym and lifting weights. So why don't you try cleaning up this house?"

When Rod again went back to Michigan, he checked in every day to see how I was doing. I started filling bags with stuff that my mom and I weren't using and carrying them down two flights of stairs from her second-floor apartment to the trash bins outside. When I left the hospital, I couldn't even walk and had to use a wheelchair. Now I was walking up and down all these flights of stairs. It was definitely making a difference.

I waited in Los Angeles for three months until one day I received the call with the sweetest words I ever heard, "We've found a donor."

> "This is recovery now!" he'd bark. "This is stew. Eat it!" And he read me the riot act about getting in better shape.

Her name was Annette Karrer, and the donor bank found her in Germany. They shipped her bone marrow to Los Angeles for the transplant. I like to say Rod is my brother and Annette is my sister.

The doctors put the new bone marrow in at 3 a.m. on May 4, 2002. The transplant was a complete success. After a three-month recovery to rebuild my immune system, I boarded a plane and finally headed back to Michigan. Guess who was there to pick me up at the airport? That's right—Rod.

I've now passed the five-year mark in great health. So doctors tell me that I'm cured.

A lot has happened since then. Rod is now married and has a baby girl. He's a high school football coach, which is the perfect job for the leadership skills he honed on me.

In so many ways we both found what we were looking for. Rod got his new life that gives him purpose postfootball. And I—well, I got life.

After all this, somehow the sportswriting career didn't seem so meaningful anymore. Now I spend my time telling our story. I've written a book, and Rod and I do a lot of public speaking. We talk about the power of friendship and the power of facing challenges with your teammates, no matter who or what the opponent is. There's no reason to face it alone.

You can learn more about Steve and Rod's story at play2inspire.com.

Daryn's Takeaways

. . . .

This story reminds me of a couple of important lessons.

One, you don't need to overcome every obstacle by yourself. Just like the Joe Cocker song says, it's good to have "a little help from my friends." I know for me, it's usually tempting to be strong and think I need to get by on my own. But often when you look up, just as Steve did that day in his hospital room, there is an awesome person willing and wanting to help you over the hump. Sometimes it pays not to be so brave and to let others in.

And I have to smile because these two "brothers" remind me that if you keep an open heart and mind, life can and will deliver you gifts in the most surprising packages. White, Jewish, sportswriter Steve could never have imagined that his best friend would show up in the form of a Super Bowl champion, African-American, Christian dynamo. And yet there was Rod to help save the day.

If nothing else, I think this is one of the most powerful questions you can take away from this book. If you let go of preconceived notions of packaging, what amazing gifts might show up in your life—or might already be there, unrecognized?

The Bald Truth

Amy Gibson,
soap opera actress

My life has been a soap opera. No, literally. I've starred in soap operas since I was 13 years old. I've also lived my own soap opera, losing my hair and hiding my secret of baldness throughout my career. When I finally lifted the wigs and looked into my heart, I found a way to touch people's hearts more deeply than any acting job could ever provide.

If you've watched soaps over the years, you'd recognize me. I played Lynn Henderson on *Love of Life*, Alana Anthony on *The Young and the Restless*, and Colette Françoise on *General Hospital* and years of different characters on prime time television. I was thriving in a superficial world because, of course, in Hollywood it's all about your looks. And at home my father supported the supreme importance of a woman's look. He used to say, "Remember, Amy, if you brush your hair 100 strokes a day, the blood will always go to the follicle and you will always have a healthy head of hair. Hair is a woman's mane—it represents her sexuality." Although I love my father, he is admittedly caught up in the external. I can't blame him for being who he is.

My mother was exactly the opposite. For her it was all about who you were inside and what you brought to the table as a human being. Thank goodness for Mom! I needed her strength and wisdom as my own soap opera began.

It was away from the cameras, in the studio makeup room, where my personal drama started. I was 13 years old, playing a troubled teen, Lynn Henderson, on *Love of Life*. At 5:30 in the morning, the hairdresser had me bend my head over and he said, "Wow, you've got a big bald spot on the back of your head."

This man was a jokester, so I thought it was some sort of gag, only this time he wasn't joking. He said, "No, no, you really need to take a look at this." He held up his hand mirror and I saw the missing patch of hair.

I started flipping out right there in the makeup room. For some reason I thought losing my hair meant I had leprosy and that my hair was just the first part of my body that would start falling off.

But it wasn't leprosy; it was alopecia. That was a word I'd never heard before. I can tell you now that alopecia is basically a technical term for hair loss or baldness. It affects 35 million people a year, women and children included. Lots of different things can cause it. And there are all different ways of dealing with it.

I went to a doctor who told me I needed to have cortisone shots injected right into the affected areas. There I was, barely a teenager and going in secretly for a series of shots. I made sure to breathe in the numbing spray they used on my head, because it blocked out what sounded like Rice Krispies popping as the painful needles entered my scalp.

I had those shots for 17 years! The cortisone screwed up my body and my emotions. My weight was up and down and I didn't enter puberty until age 17. No medical professional ever said, "What are you doing?" No one ever thought about it. It was just what you did to keep hair and stay pretty. I was so afraid that someone would find out I was bald and that I would be ousted from the industry. So I just kept quiet and kept getting the shots.

Finally, after about 20 years a turn in my career provided an opportunity to start changing how I looked at my baldness. I was actually in the middle of a career dry spell. It had been a couple of years since I wrapped up *The Young and the Restless*. Money was tight, so I was thrilled to get a call from the producers at *General Hospital*. Not only did they have a job for me, they were creating a fabulous part of an undercover detective named Colette Françoise. I took the part; they didn't even test me; they just gave me the role. That's when I started freaking out.

Because money was short, I had been skipping the cortisone treatments and I had a ton of bald spots. But now I really had to get the shots because I only had eight weeks to grow back some hair. The doctor that day gave me so much cortisone that when I walked out of the office I was suddenly seeing double. I even had an anxiety attack right there on the sidewalk. My body was telling me, "No more!" So I stopped all treatment, and within three weeks all of my hair was gone. I was completely bald.

> There is something about a woman losing her hair that makes her feel like she's losing her femininity.

Aside from what this did to my self-esteem as a young woman, I was panicking that I would lose this job. Shooting would begin in just five weeks. As I told you—drama! That's when my mom's words came back to me: "Remember, Amy, a woman can move mountains with her mind." I had to turn this situation around, so I came up with a wild idea for the soap character. I would turn this detective into one with seven different dialects and seven different looks to get her man. That, of course, meant she would have to wear a number of different wigs.

I pitched the idea to the producer and he loved it. "Amy!" he shrieked. "This is amazing! The network is going to love it! What made you think of this?" he wanted to know.

I had no choice. This would be the first time I would share my secret, but he was sensitive and compassionate, so I felt safe to move forward with my plan. "And to make this work right, we need the network to pay for $100,000 in really good wigs." The producer stood by me and the network invested in the story line, and it was a success.

Still I kept my secret from almost everyone else. As I looked into support groups and did more research, I realized I wasn't alone. Slowly but surely I started to share, sometimes in surprising ways.

One woman said to me, "I really like your hair." Of course, she didn't realize she was admiring my wig.

"Really?" I replied. "You can have it too because I don't have any."

She looked at me, dazed, and asked, "What's that supposed to mean?"

"It means exactly what I said. I don't have any hair."

She replied, "I don't have any either."

Now she was the one who surprised me because she was wearing a hat and I saw her hair coming out at the sides. "Yes, you do," I insisted.

But she took off the hat, and her head was completely bald on top. She told me she always wore a hat because she couldn't find a decent wig.

Now, I had access to good wig makers, and at that moment it hit me how difficult it was for a woman who doesn't have $5,000 to $10,000 to spend to find a good wig. I asked this woman, "Where are you getting some support for dealing with your hair loss?"

She said, "Nowhere."

The next week I ran into somebody else with a similar problem. Within three months I was inundated with calls from women dealing with baldness. I realized there were signs all around me: This was the real life part I was meant to play.

And that's how Crown and Glory Enterprises was born. We consult with women and girls suffering from hair loss, and over the years I have learned how to design top-quality custom-made human hair wigs that are designed for comfort. And working with International Hairgoods Inc., I developed a line of wigs called Amy's Presence that is distributed throughout the United States and internationally. We make all sorts of wigs for all sorts of lifestyles, everything from our Swim Wig to our Intimacy Wig. My R Secret Bag has all the goodies you need to keep your wig fresh for those spontaneous times when you're on the run.

I love sharing all the tricks I've learned over the years. But most of all I love the work I'm able to do with the hearts and souls of my clients and friends. There is something about a woman losing her hair that makes her feel like she's losing her femininity. I help women realize we are more than our hair. I empower them to know there are things they can do to make themselves feel whole. They are not alone. When you feel alone, you stop searching. But if you know you're not alone, you look for other women and you look for answers.

I learn from every client. I now take on clients as young as 4 years old. A beautiful 10-year-old girl with unexplained baldness looked at me one day and said, "Oh, Amy, we're so smart that our brains can't hold on to our hair!" Brilliant! I love my little ones!

Sixty percent of my business is now chemotherapy patients who are about to lose their hair. For them my job is providing support and education before they lose their hair and helping them find a calmer approach to this process in the interim, which can be devastating. I then provide comfortable alternatives for them to turn to when their hair grows back. And I help them think about when it's OK to take the wig off and be comfortable with short hair if that's what they want.

I counsel them. They inspire me. I'll never forget one young mother, eight months pregnant with her second child when she was diagnosed with Stage 3 breast cancer. She came to me the Friday before she was going to have a cesarean section, have both breasts removed, and begin chemo.

All she wanted me to do was help her get a wig so that she could look normal and get through what was coming. "Amy," she said, "I don't care about any of this. They can take any part of my body. Just help me get through this so that I can be there for my children."

It's people like that who show me the best way past any obstacle is to say, "I have plans beyond this." These courageous women have also convinced me how small my own problems really are at times.

I see every day that I'm on a very important mission. Acting was great, but I never felt in alignment. I always felt there was something more. Finally I know I'm playing exactly the role I'm meant to play.

You can find out more at amyspresence.com.

An Orchard Full of Good People

Mary Anne Tillman,
wife, mother, and proud dog owner

When my husband and our dog were struck by a hit-and-run driver, I was outraged. My anger fueled a campaign to find that one bad apple. Instead our family found healing and a whole orchard of wonderful people.

First, as a proud dog owner, I have to brag about our beloved Ozzie. He's a 4-year-old Airedale terrier. Admittedly he's not the world's best-behaved dog, but he's the absolute love of our entire family.

My daughter and I saw him in a local pet store and knew we had to have him. My husband, Ziggy, wasn't so sure. He said we didn't need the dog. But from the moment we brought him home, it has been clear—Ozzie is Ziggy's dog. He waits for him to get home each night and spends the evening staring at my husband with eyes full of love. When Ziggy is sitting in a chair, Ozzie is right there beside him with his paw up on Ziggy's leg. I've never seen anything like it. Ziggy calls Ozzie his best friend.

It was a typical fall night in October 2006 when Ziggy grabbed the leash and took Ozzie out for their evening walk. On this particular night Ziggy decided to walk Ozzie a bit farther because I had missed his morning walk. They were just a few blocks from our home in Glenolden, Pennsylvania, when all of a sudden my husband heard a noise.

"The next thing I knew," he told me, "We were on the grass. I was holding Ozzie, who was yelping and crying. I looked up the road and saw a little black car stop about 50 yards down the block. But then it took off. That's when I realized our dog saved my life. Ozzie, all 90 pounds of him, had taken the brunt of the impact between the car and me. I had a few bumps and bruises, but he took the hit for me by stepping between me and the car."

It was clear right away that the protection had come at a high price, although we didn't realize how badly Ozzie was hurt until we took him to the vet. He had a bruised lung, a dislocated hip, an anklebone that was sanded down to the ligaments, and a 5-inch gash across his leg. They also found a piece of the car's headlight embedded in Ozzie's face.

All the injuries meant he had to spend more than two weeks in the hospital. As Ozzie healed, the vet bills quickly added up to well over $5,000. We honestly didn't think he was going to survive and weren't sure how we were going to pay those vet bills.

> By the time we met the woman in court, we were a very different family.

Meanwhile, our family went on a mission to find the hit-and-run driver. We were so angry and hurt, and on top of that we were frustrated and depressed because Ozzie was in a part of the vet hospital we weren't allowed to visit. We couldn't do anything for him, so we focused on finding the bad guy.

We put up posters that read "Justice For Ozzie!" We called television stations and newspapers to put the word out to help us find what we believed to be a terrible person. This was during election season, so we also put flyers in the offices of all the people running for re-election.

Actually my daughter and I did most of this work. My husband is a proud man who has never asked anyone for help. It didn't occur to him that somebody might do exactly that. I believed, however, that someone must have seen something that could help us find the driver.

As we focused on the hunt for this person, the most amazing thing happened. Strangers started sending money to help with Ozzie's vet bills, calling to express their sympathy, and praying for us. Strangers were dropping off dog supplies and toys. It never occurred to us that people would send us money and gifts. That's never what our crusade was about.

One woman called the house to tell me her husband had given her $300 for their anniversary and she wanted to donate it to Ozzie. When she wouldn't take no for answer, I thanked her profusely and asked for her name and address so I could at least send her a thank-you note. "Oh, no, please don't," she asked. "I don't want my husband to know this is what I did with my gift money!"

Soon it was clear that Ozzie's vet bills would be covered. We used an additional $40 to buy Ozzie a new bed and some toys. And still the donations kept coming! Our sweet Ozzie was not only our hero, he was becoming a philanthropist. We set up the Ozzie Tillman Fund for the extra donations, which would be used to treat other dogs whose owners didn't have the means to pay their vet bills.

Ozzie certainly had his own challenges to overcome. After two weeks in the hospital, he had to wear a leg cast for five months. Even after he healed physically, he appeared to have lost his desire to go on any walks at all. We had to bring in a dog trainer to teach him it would be OK and safe to enjoy walks again.

On one of the visits to the vet, I met a wonderful woman, Kelly, who had rescued and was fostering a little 5-month-old shepherd-mix puppy named Freddie who had been left out on the streets of Philadelphia. Freddie, too, had been hit by a car and received no medical attention, so he had an old pelvic and leg injury. The shelter told his foster mom she could take him back to the shelter and have him euthanized, but Kelly wouldn't do it.

I asked the vet to use some of the Ozzie Fund to help with Freddie's medical bills. Today Freddie is fully healed, and his foster mom has adopted him.

With all this goodness going around, we weren't prepared when one night the police knocked on the door. "I have news about one of your kids," the officer said. At first we were terrified that something had happened to our son or daughter. But the officer then said, "We've made an arrest in Ozzie's hit-and-run case." The driver turned out to be a 30-year-old woman who said her boyfriend had been distracting her and told her to drive off after the collision. The body shop working on the damaged car was able to match a piece of the headlight taken from Ozzie's face to the car, helping crack the case.

By the time we met the woman face-to-face in court, we were a very different family. It was clear that Ozzie was going to survive, and our anger had been transformed by the overwhelming, unexpected kindness of strangers.

That's why I was able to look this woman in the eye and forgive her. This was her first offense, and she clearly knew she had made a big mistake. I could see she wasn't intentionally gunning for Ozzie and Ziggy that night. I told her that everyone makes mistakes and that she needed to grow and move on from hers. I also shared with her all the amazing good that had come from that night.

Her car insurance company stepped up and paid all of Ozzie's vet bills, which in the end totaled about $17,000. That meant the $20,000 that came in from strangers could all be donated to other animal funds. Our own vet spent her share saving a German shepherd puppy born with a birth defect. We donated thousands to the Airedale and St. Bernard Rescue Leagues, and some of the funds paid for a new police dog puppy and its training.

I hope the driver sees that good things can come out of bad situations.

As for Ozzie, I'm pleased to say he is completely healed. He and Ziggy are back to their old routine of evening walks, although now he goes with a special leash that lights up so drivers can see him more easily. Not surprising, they don't go down the road where the collision took place. Other than that, their love affair has not missed a beat.

Our family has learned so much. We learned that even a dog that is not normally the best-behaved dog on the block can become a hero. We learned it's a good idea to ask for help. And most important, we learned you might go looking for one bad apple, but the world is actually an orchard full of good people.

Part 3

. . . .

Dreaming Big: In Pursuit of a Passion

A 21-Year Lesson Plan

Sharon Hayes-Brown,
full-time mother and college graduate

It took me 21 years, 10 months, and 1 day to get my college degree. Four rambunctious kids, a husband, and a demanding life don't mix well with college. Part of my education was learning to struggle for it.

In the fall of 1985, I was a bright-eyed Connecticut girl heading off to Howard University in Washington, D.C., aiming at a legal career and dreaming of sitting on a Supreme Court bench somewhere. Twenty-one years later I am still a bright-eyed dreamer but one with quite a different tale to tell.

Let me first tell you about my grandmother. In 1986 she graduated from college at the age of 65. She was the first person in our family to reach that goal—talk about an amazing role model. I remember her graduation day. My grandmother showed me it's never too late to go after your dream. Through no fault of her own, she also derailed my life course drastically.

One year after I started college, just after my grandmother earned her degree, she developed cancer. I made the choice to withdraw from college to care for her. I will never regret the time I spent with my grandmother, but it did mean that school and my personal dream would have to wait.

Before I left the university, a special young man caught my eye. Tommy Brown and I believed we were going to conquer the world. We married in 1991.

We moved around to several places, including Georgia and Pennsylvania. When we finally settled in Charlotte, North Carolina, I thought it was time to get back to that personal dream of my undergraduate degree. As it turned out, that personal dream would have to wait.

Tommy and I had another dream: building our family. Ever since I was a teenager, I knew I wanted to build my family with a combination of adopted and biological children. Just seeing how many African-American children were languishing in foster care and how there weren't many African-American families either able or willing to adopt made us decide to be a family that did adopt.

Tommy and I received the phone call in July 1999.

"We've got some news. I think we have a baby boy for you."

Two days later we went and picked up our son sight unseen. His name is Oree Believe. Oree is the last name of Tommy's grandfather, a wonderful man who had a strong influence on Tommy's upbringing. Oree's middle name, Believe, is self-explanatory.

To lay eyes on him was incredible—and very emotional. It was one of the happiest days of my life. Of course, any new mother would understand that my dream of going back to school full-time would have to wait.

Almost a year later we received another call from the adoption agency. They said, "We have another little boy for you if you're interested."

That's when we welcomed Zion Zebari into our family.

Zion means "the place where God dwells." *Zebari* is the Swahili word for "strong." Born two months premature and in intensive care for the first two months of his life, Zion overcame great odds just to survive.

It was also love at first sight with our second son. Still, taking care of two little ones, including one in the hospital, meant full-time college would again have to wait.

We thought we were just going to have two boys. But then, yes, you guessed it. The phone rang again in 2002, and there came son No. 3. His name is Isiah Jisani. *Jisani* is another Swahili word, meaning "child of the sun."

By this time Tommy and I realized that if we were ever going to fit a biological child into this mix, we had better go ahead and do it.

In November 2003, I gave birth to, of course, another boy! That's our sweet Solomon Soul.

Often people will say to us, "Oh, so you adopted three children and had one of your own." We are very quick to tell them we have four of our own. I say it all the time. They don't share the same blood, but they share the same parents. They're brothers in every sense of the word. But I've gotten off track here. This story started with my telling you about my dream to get my college degree. (This story is like my life!) You can imagine how crammed my life had become, raising four boys under the age of 8! Our family was complete and our home was a complete zoo. A joyous zoo, to be sure. Not surprising, I never did make it back to college full-time. But I never gave up on the dream either. Honestly there was never enough time or money for me to go back to school.

> Let me assure you, I am not special. I was just single-minded. You can have it all if you're patient and willing to work at things.

I had only one choice: to find a way. Usually that meant taking as few as one class each semester. But you know what? You do that enough semesters and those classes start to add up. Just as we built our family one son at a time, I tackled my degree one class at a time.

The hardest part was feeling guilty about the time I spent away from the boys. I went to school at night, so I involved the kids with my education; as they studied, I studied too. I worked on projects after they went to bed.

There certainly were times I wanted to quit. Fortunately I was too far in. I also could hear my parents' voices in my head. They were not college educated, and they always insisted college was something we must do. They understood the value of an education. That meant for me education was a nonnegotiable priority.

The kids often wanted me to stay home with them, but I knew they learned by watching me. I showed them there is no such thing as "can't." In fact in our home they aren't allowed to use that word. I believe that rather than selfishly taking time away from them, I gave them a role model that will take them through the rest of their lives.

In 2007 I graduated from the University of North Carolina at Charlotte with a double major in African studies and communication, with a minor in journalism. It took me over 21 years!

Let me assure you, I am not special. I was just single-minded. It always struck me that when you're looking at a big challenge from the outside it looks enormous, but when you're in the midst of it, it just seems normal.

I often hear people say that you can't have it all. It's been my experience that you *can* have it all if you're patient and willing to work at things. Everything you want won't arrive in your life on one day. It's a process, and if you accept that things take time and that they require focus, you can have nearly anything.

Yes, anything! That includes a college degree. Earning my undergraduate degree has inspired another dream. I will soon be starting my master's degree in creative writing.

How will I find time for that? I'll find a way because I know little steps add up to big dreams.

Daryn's Takeaways

Sharon's story reminds me of a saying, "Life is what happens when you're busy making plans."

Many of her plans unfolded just the way she dreamed they would as she and her husband built their beautiful family. But twentysomething Sharon surely never dreamed it would take her another 20 years to fulfill her goal of getting her college degree.

The diploma she has today is no less valuable than the one she could have earned two decades ago. In fact I have no doubt she cherishes it even more.

It's not the journey she thought she would take to accomplish it. But at some point Sharon was willing to let go of trying to control exactly how her dream would be realized without giving up on the dream itself.

I have found that lesson so valuable in my own life. When I let go of preconceived notions of what something is supposed to look like or how and when it is supposed to appear, reality usually outdoes my own imagination.

Which accomplishments and dreams would be possible in your life if you let go of your preconceived idea of what it is supposed to look like or when it's supposed to arrive?

Lifting the Heaviest of Dreams

Melanie Roach,
champion weightlifter

There aren't a lot of 5-foot-tall women who can lift double their body weight above their head. But that's exactly what I do. It's all part of living my dream and making sports history. To all the folks with back trouble and all the mothers out there: It's never too late to go for your dreams!

Look at me casually and you'll see a diminutive woman with three small children running around, a husband who is a state legislator in the great state of Washington, and a family-run gymnastics school in Bonney Lake, Washington.

Hang around a little longer and you'll come with me to international weightlifting events where I hold a total of 400 pounds and more above my head. Let me do some math for you: I stand 5 feet tall and I weigh 117 pounds. And yes, I get the biggest rush from picking up those hundreds of pounds of dumbbells!

To give you a brief primer on the sport: There are two events, the Snatch and the Clean and Jerk. The woman with the biggest combined total wins. My best competition lifts are the Snatch at 79 kilos (173 pounds), the Clean and Jerk at 110 kilos (242 pounds), and the best total: 189 kilos (416 pounds). Not bad for a washed-up small-town gymnast.

Gymnastics was the first sport I fell in love with at age 12. I started training with the dream of one day going to the Olympics. In retrospect I can see I had no chance: Olympic gymnasts start when they're tiny girls. But you don't tell a determined 12-year-old she's not going to the Olympics!

I worked hard at training, but when I dislocated my elbow in a high school gymnastics meet, it meant reconstructive surgery and the end of my Olympic dreams. That was a huge disappointment but also the first time I would see that when one door closes, another one opens.

The door didn't open right away, however. I went off to college and did the typical drill of gaining weight and letting myself get out of shape. I didn't even think of myself as an athlete anymore. But the summer after my freshman year, I ran into an old friend. She was now on a weightlifting team and asked me if I wanted to join.

I had a picture in my mind of what female weightlifters looked like. It was nothing like the look I wanted. I said, "No way!"

The next summer I ran into the same girl again. And once more she invited me to check out the gym where she lifted weights. By this point I was even more out of shape and I thought, "Maybe I should try this."

It was April 1994. I went out on a Saturday afternoon and instantly fell in love with weightlifting. I was sure I didn't want to compete; I just wanted to get back in shape. So much for the best-laid plans! By June I had entered my first competition and actually qualified for the American Open. At the time, I didn't know what a huge opportunity this was for me. It created a life lesson for the first half of my career—learning never to take success for granted. The problem was that in fact I had other priorities—such as a boyfriend who had a boat and lived on the lake. I blew off weightlifting again, and although I had lots of talent (that I underappreciated), it stagnated.

Thank goodness one of the most important people in my life wouldn't leave me alone. His name is John Thrush and he is one of the best weightlifting coaches in the world. He happened to live right down the road. He kept calling me, and at his urging I agreed to get serious about weightlifting and go to the American Open. Lo and behold, I placed third.

The next few years were a blur of great weightlifting success and great failure in my personal life.

I won my first national championship in 1997 when I was still in my early twenties. I had been married during this time but it was slowly fizzling out, something I never thought possible. To be truthful, the relationship was rocky before I restarted my weightlifting. But it was over, and I divorced that year.

With that emotional battle behind me, my career as a weightlifter took off. I also met a wonderful man who would not only support my weightlifting in crucial moments but over the next eight years would also become my husband and the father of my three beautiful children. And I was still weightlifting!

It wasn't all rosy. I had achieved worldwide recognition for lifting in my weight class, but the problems began almost immediately. My husband was facing bitter challenges to his political ambitions (he actually lost his first election just prior to our marriage), we would soon be starting a family, I hyperextended my elbow in the Pan American Games in the late 1990s (requiring six weeks of rehab), and developed a herniated disk in my back just eight weeks before the Olympic trials—all the while running a gymnastics program!

I was busy, and things weren't going well. In fact I was devastated athletically because I missed my shot at my dream: the Olympics. I bombed out at the trials due to my injuries and returned to Washington a defeated soul.

I tried to watch the Olympics that year and cheer on other friends as they were living their dream. I wanted to be there with them so badly. I couldn't take the sadness, so I turned off the TV and didn't watch a moment of the Olympics that year. But turning off the TV is easier than turning off your dreams.

I thought about a comeback after the birth of each child. Finally, after the birth of our third child, I decided it was now or never. I was in my early thirties and I found I had more than age working against me.

The first challenge my husband and I never saw coming. Our younger son, Drew, was diagnosed with autism. As a devoted mom I was devastated, and I spent the better part of that summer establishing an extensive therapy program for him. I also had to come to grips with the fact that our sweet boy may never go to high school dances, do a mission for our church, get married, or live out the other dreams we had for him.

I went through a mourning process when I discovered my child had a disability. I also learned some important lessons from raising a special-needs child. I learned to celebrate the potential for his life and to appreciate what I have—something I never learned in all those years I was winning awards and accolades in the early part of my weightlifting career.

So back to the gym and competition I went. You should have seen the looks on some of the competitors' faces when I showed up at the trials for the Pan American Championships. It was like, "Where did this old lady come from?" I'll tell you where I was going—to the championships.

Yes, I made the team. I also had to face a serious problem. My back pain was getting worse. Sometimes I couldn't even stand up as pain shot from my back down into my knees.

I almost quit three or four times, but my amazing chiropractor kept me going. I also benefited from some cutting-edge back surgery. Within weeks of the operation, I was lifting again. I won the bronze medal at the Pan Am Games in June 2007.

In many ways my comeback is complete. I've been able to re-create much of the success I had in my early twenties, only this time around I appreciate every moment of the experience. I still hunger for that big dream that eluded me, even at the height of my earlier success—the Olympics.

The trials are held in early 2008. If I qualify, you'll see my personal comeback story played out on TV in Beijing. It will be the culmination of a dream for me and, I hope, a true inspiration for you.

I'm just an ordinary woman, a wife and mother who believes that if you want something, you can find a way. I know you probably don't want to lift twice your body weight above your head. That's OK. But if you have a dream you've wished for, start today and get busy. It just might be closer than you think.

My Head in the Clouds

Kent Couch,
cluster balloon aviator

I've been called "nuts," "crazy," even a "balloon-atic." But I don't care because I've done something most people will never have the nerve to do. I made my boyhood dream come true. I flew through the sky—by attaching a bunch of helium balloons to a lawn chair.

I'm a husband, father of five, and a minimart gas station owner in Bend, Oregon. I swear I'm no daredevil or extreme sports guy. Even motorcycles and roller coasters scare me as too dangerous. So I might be the last guy to try something wild like floating away on a lawn chair attached to helium balloons.

Ever since I was a kid, I've fantasized about how peaceful it must be up in the clouds. Remember lying on your back in your yard looking up at the big poofy clouds? Just about every child dreams about flying through the clouds like Superman or on a magic carpet. Most kids let go of their childhood dreams as they grow up and take on the responsibilities of families and career. I never did.

Sometime in 2006 I was watching a TV program about a man named Larry Walters. He was the first one to figure out how to attach helium balloons to a lawn chair and make the contraption fly. Walters did it in 1982 and he has long since died of unrelated causes. As I watched that

story I thought, "Well, goodness! If it can be done, why am I not doing it?!" Here it was, my chance to float among the clouds.

Of course, I first had to check with my wife. She's incredible and supports me in whatever I want to do. Looking back, I think she probably didn't believe I was entirely serious and thought that if she didn't make a fuss, I would forget about it. She was wrong.

My partner in this adventure was my good friend, Kimi Feuer. I'm obviously the "pie in the sky" dreamer. Kimi is very analytical and helped me figure out the engineering end of things.

First we had to figure out how many balloons we needed. I didn't want a big hot air balloon. I wanted a bouquet, so we decided no balloon would be more than 4 to 5 feet in diameter. Then we bought a bottle of helium, filled up one balloon, and tied a water bucket to the bottom. By measuring the weight of the water, we figured out that each balloon could lift 5 pounds.

The next step was learning how to sky dive. I would need to know how to parachute out of the lawn chair if things went wrong. The skydiving instructors were some of my harshest critics. They all warned me I shouldn't try this. And these were guys who jump out of planes every day! I didn't appreciate their lack of encouragement, mainly because they didn't even ask *how* I was planning to do this to see if I had thought it through.

There were other critics too. But I'll bet the Wright Brothers or Thomas Edison or anyone else who took a big leap had critics. It probably didn't seem like an extreme risk to them.

The harshest criticism came from my youngest daughter, who was away at college. She told me I was being irresponsible and selfish. She actually refused to come home to help with the first flight. I admit it; that one hit hard. Like the skydiving instructors, if she simply had listened, I could have explained how well I believed I had thought out the plan.

The day of my first flight came quickly. We rigged up the lawn chair to 57 balloons. We needed that many to lift about 500 pounds: me, the chair, the parachute, and various other pieces of equipment. Camping jugs filled with water hung from the side of the chair to act as the ballast.

Off I went into the early morning Oregon sky. Talk about a dream come true! It was just like I had imagined as a kid, only better. I had such an incredible feeling of pure peacefulness. Floating up there in my lawn chair felt like my magic carpet ride. I didn't feel any wind since I was floating with the wind. There was obviously no propeller, so it was very quiet. We hadn't built any steering into the chair, so I rotated at the whim of the wind, sometimes facing north, sometimes south, west, or east.

I made it up to 12,000 feet! When I wanted to come down a bit to catch better wind, I simply shot one of the balloons out with a BB gun. If I wanted to go back up, I released some of the water from the jugs. That made me lighter so the balloons took me higher.

To be completely honest, this flight did have its challenges. When I rose past 12,000 feet up to 15,000 feet, the pressure of the elevation made six of the balloons pop, so I began to descend. But then the morning sun came up over the horizon, heating the ground. That made the balloons rise again. And again more balloons popped—this time seven. As I started to fall, I did some math. I had started with 57; 13 were gone. I was dropping about 7 feet per second. I knew I had to think about landing.

I radioed back to Kimi and my chase team. I told them I either had to drop weight by throwing my parachute over or use the parachute and jump. Kimi made the call. "I think you better use the parachute," he recommended.

So that's what I did; I jumped off the lawn chair at 2,200 feet. Good thing I took those skydiving lessons. Despite what those instructors warned, I landed just fine in a cow pasture.

The lawn chair didn't fare as well. As soon as I jumped, the balloons shot straight up into the sky. The balloons and lawn chair have never been heard from since.

Overall I was thrilled with the experience. Kimi and I figured we learned so much from the first flight that we had to send me up again. The second time we used a reclining lawn chair for more comfort, more balloons for more lift, and more water in the jugs for more elevation control. The improvements helped, and I flew 100 miles farther than the first time.

Again I had the time of my life. This time was extra special because my doubting daughter was now along for the launch. Since she had seen how well the first flight went, she wanted to be part of the chase team.

Unfortunately we again lost the balloons and lawn chair at the end of the flight. This time I bailed while flying just a few feet above the ground. And again, with the lack of weight the contraption took off. We're actually offering a $500 reward if anyone happens to come across a lawn chair with a bunch of deflated helium balloons attached.

> It was just like I had imagined as a kid, only better. Floating up there in my lawn chair felt like my magic carpet ride.

I'm not done. My dream is to one day fly across the open plains of Australia. Some people don't understand that, just like they don't understand my original dream. But here's what I know: Everyone has a kid inside with dreams from long ago—even the most businesslike professionals.

We're only in this world once. The time is now to make those dreams come true. Of course, cluster ballooning isn't for everyone, but whatever your dream is, forget the critics and go for it. Just don't call me to watch if it's motorcycles or roller coasters. That would scare me to no end!

For more on Kent Couch's cluster balloon flights, check out couchballoons.com.

Daryn's Takeaways

Hold everything! I don't want all of you to go tie a bunch of balloons to the lawn chair in your yard! But I do appreciate the way Kent is able to hold on to his childhood dream and his sense of whimsy.

What did you daydream about when you were a kid? What dream would you still like to make come true?

Painting Myself Out of a Corner

Dan Dunn,
performance artist and YouTube phenomenon

As a 45-year-old artist who had explored many art forms in a career spanning decades, I was in a rut. I had a background in painting and illustration but made my living drawing caricatures at events. This paid well, but not enough to pay for my family's expanding financial needs. We were $40,000 in the hole! My story shows what can happen when you take a chance, try something new—and tap into your kids' computer life.

I have been an artist all my life. I love to draw and spent my school days sitting in the back of the class drawing and sketching. School was a struggle though, and I even flunked ninth grade. Although totally humiliating, this turned out to be the best thing that ever happened to me.

My father owned a job placement service for executives. He had me tested by his former psychology professor, and it turned out that my spatial reasoning, abstract understanding, and color sense placed me in the 97th percentile in the nation in art. The good doctor's verdict: "Send the kid to art school and get off his back!"

This was a milestone, a turning point in my life. I enrolled as an art major at Sam Houston State University. As soon as I met my professors, I knew I was among "my people" and had found my life's work.

As a sophomore in college, I took a summer job as a caricature artist at a theme park, Six Flags Astroworld in Houston. I took home a whopping 25 percent of the gross sales—50 cents a sketch. My caricature experience at the theme park soon led to drawing for events, company picnics, and trade shows all over the country. I would sit for hours with a line of eager guests waiting for their turn to be drawn. I would work a company picnic in the morning in 90° weather with no breeze, then work a bar mitzvah that night. During prom season I would then do a project from midnight until 4 a.m. and then be at another picnic at 11 Sunday morning.

> In many ways I had it made, but I felt unfulfilled as an artist. I wasn't painting what I wanted, only what was requested.

Along the way I also worked in the advertising business, and for a time I was employed as a toy designer at a toy company. In 1989 I started my own caricature company for events and won national awards for my work—second in the nation in 1993 and third in 1994, when I competed for Caricaturist of the Year with the National Caricaturist Network.

In many ways I had it made. I was making a living with art, my family life was great, and I had wonderful friends. But I felt unfulfilled as an artist. I was not painting what I wanted or what I found interesting, only what was requested.

My friends from Astroworld had gone on to bigger things. One was a background painter for Disney. One had done comic books and illustration for George Lucas' *Star Wars* franchise. Another had become a writer whose credits included David Letterman, Drew Carey, *The Simpsons*, Disney, and the WB. Yet there I was, still working the Houston party circuit, practicing a craft I had learned 30 years ago. As the kids got older, we were feeling more financial pressure, even though I was the most successful caricaturist in a city of 4 million people and was working over 200 events per year.

There was no doubt about it: I was having a midlife crisis.

Years earlier I had been blown away by the great performance artist

Denny Dent. Denny did large paintings on stage to rock music. I thought, "Whoa! This guy has invented a new form of rock and roll." Denny passed away in 2004, and that seemed like an open door to me.

The best way to describe what I do on stage is this: I create a finished painting on a 6- to 8-foot canvas in as little as two to seven minutes. I paint in such a way that it looks abstract until the final 30 seconds, when I place a few final touches and reveal a detailed portrait of Ray Charles or John Lennon or Lady Liberty. I look like a crazy person, throwing paint, frantically using brushes and bare hands while rock music blasts away in the background. It's magic, and audiences gasp when I reveal the image. It is also very aerobic. I have lost 15 pounds and put on muscle since I started the show.

I knew that rehearsal was the key to getting this act down. I needed a big space where I could throw paint. A warehouse would have been perfect, but I was $40,000 in debt, so I went shopping for mini-warehouse storage space. The first six didn't want me "occupying" the space; it was for storage only. At the seventh facility the owner agreed to let me lease a space. It was 13 by 15 feet, about as big as the back of a moving van.

I covered the walls and ceiling in plastic and covered the floor with some carpet I found in a Dumpster. I bought a laptop computer for sound and a small, inexpensive PA system. For lighting I used $5 clip-on lights from the hardware store with 100-watt bulbs. No frills.

There was no restroom. I washed brushes in a bucket filled from a garden hose out back, but it was wonderful because I was on an artistic adventure! I loved it and would squeeze in every precious hour that I could here and there, week by week, to practice.

When I finished my first huge painting, I stepped back and could see the simple, bright effect of my palette—blue, purple, yellow. It took my breath away! It was intoxicating! The whole process of throwing myself at my art, using my bare hands, getting covered in paint, getting it in my hair, sometimes in my eyes or my mouth was very satisfying.

We booked our first show on the Fourth of July at a festival. We had a huge response. We were on our way! We started getting bookings locally and after three years were doing several shows a month. Then through our web page we landed a booking in a variety show in Atlantic City for a two-week run.

All along the way, we knew that this venture was the most successful thing we have ever done. I speak in the plural because my wife and kids are right there with me working as road crew, helping in the studio, and going with me on local events. My 20-year-old son, Matt, is now my road manager and handles logistics, sound, lighting. So we were starting to have modest success.

Then came YouTube.

I decided to post a video of the Atlantic City show online. I logged on to YouTube, and when I did I accidentally posted my video on my 13-year-old daughter's page. I corrected my mistake and made my own page but left the videos on her page. As my biggest fan, she started spreading the word on her MySpace account.

That's when the craziness began. The phone started ringing with event planners, corporations, and producers contacting us to book our show. I was surprised because my page had only had a few hundred hits in a month. "I saw you on YouTube," they would say. "You've had 25,000 hits." I was stunned. Then I realized they were looking at it on my daughter's page! It grew day by day, and after eight weeks we'd had 10 million views.

We were in the top 50 most viewed videos, and life has not been the same since. I have a manager with two assistants to wade through all of the offers. He is with the largest entertainment agency in Canada, which also represents Norah Jones and Howie Mandel. My bookings are taking me across the country and to Europe. I've gone from two gigs a month to three and four gigs a week in a different city every few days, and my fee has increased tenfold.

It's amazing after all these years to be comfortable financially. We try not to be extravagant, but now if we want something we can say, "Why not?" I love being able to be generous.

Most of all, I am having a blast. I started by helping my family, but I also intend to do good things with my fame and wealth as they build.

I especially hope to find ways to raise awareness about art and artists. I sure know what it is to struggle, and I hope I can help others with their journey.

It has been quite a ride to see what the magic of the Internet has done for my painting show. If I hadn't taken the risk and decided to try something new with my career, none of this would have happened. That and the love and faith of my family behind me, supporting me, have made it all possible.

If you are halfway through your life thinking, "There has to be something more," then I encourage you to go for it. But first you have to be willing to change the way you paint your picture. The big reveal of your new chapter makes all the risk and change worth it.

You can see Dan Dunn's work and his performances at paintjam.com.

Composing My Dream Orchestra

Alondra de la Parra,
conductor and 26-year-old founder of the
Philharmonic Orchestra of the Americas

I am the first woman from Mexico to conduct a professional orchestra in New York City. I got the opportunity at the age of 24 by creating the orchestra myself!

I grew up in Mexico City surrounded by classical music. It feels like I grew up in a concert hall, listening to music, watching dance, and going to the theater. I also studied piano and music composition.

Even when I was a little girl, I would watch the performances with crazy ideas of how it could be better. "Why do the musicians look so bored?" I wondered. "Why is there this stiff disconnection between the performers and the audience? This music is so beautiful and fantastic. It shouldn't be like that."

My questioning of things in the classical music world took me on a journey I could never have expected.

When I was 19 I came to New York City to study at the Manhattan School of Music. Even while I had this incredible opportunity and challenge to study with the world's best, I was still asking questions.

Why was so much of the classical music that is performed in New York City focused on European composers, I wondered. Of course, that music is beautiful. It is the mother of classical music, but it is the same music performed over and over again.

I dreamed of an orchestra or a platform where people could experience the wonderful classical music I knew from Mexico and Central and South America.

Making my dream come true started with a single concert. The Consulate of Mexico asked me to put together a group of performers featuring music from Mexico. They were thinking small, maybe a few musicians. I had a bigger vision.

I put together a 65-piece orchestra and booked New York City's Town Hall. I found sponsors to underwrite the event, and it was a huge success. The audience loved it, and the orchestra received good reviews.

That's when my mentor, Ken Kiesler, upped the challenge. After this big night, he looked at me and said, "You're crazy if you think this is a one-time thing. Look at everything you achieved with this one concert. You need to create this as a real orchestra."

I said, "Sure," but truthfully I had no idea what I was getting myself into. I needed a board of directors, I needed to become an official nonprofit organization, and I needed a lot of money. All this while I was still going to school full-time.

I did it the way you play a piece of music, one note at a time. First I organized a little concert fundraiser with a core group of six or seven musicians who have been with me from the beginning. We played for free, and the audiences gave me great feedback.

Then we did another concert and another. In three years we went from raising $50,000 to $1 million.

The time commitment was unbelievable. There were no weekends or vacations. My music studies and this orchestra became my entire life.

There were times I thought, "This is crazy!" and I became discouraged. That feeling would last maybe five or six minutes, then something incredible would happen. I would get an email from someone offering funding. Or one of the musicians would come up with a great idea. It's like the orchestra and the inspiration refused to die. That kept me going.

Some people might think I was crazy to start an orchestra in my early twenties. But I've heard from critics about my age before. When I was young and serious about my piano studies, someone told me I was too old to begin piano when I did.

But as I became a successful pianist, I began to realize that anything is possible if I put my mind to it. And criticism? Well, that is just one person's opinion. It doesn't mean it's real. So I didn't go around listening to a lot of doubting people's opinions.

I also learned that hard work will always take you somewhere good. If you work really hard trying to achieve plan A and you're not that good at it, you might not get that exact dream come true. But you will get plan B or C, something better that you didn't even know was going to come along.

> I've learned that hard work will always take you somewhere good. It may not be your exact dream come true, but something better.

What has come with the Philharmonic Orchestra of the Americas has been amazing. We have performed eight concerts and have just completed our first successful international tour, debuting in Mexico City, Dallas, and Washington, D.C.'s Kennedy Center for the Performing Arts to great acclaim.

And I've made sure that the audience has the kind of classical music experience I've always wanted. I talk to the audience; I engage them. I want them to feel connected and not just come to a hall, passively watch some bored-looking musicians, and go home.

I see the mission of this orchestra as bringing the phenomenal classical music of Mexico and Central and South America to a new audience. I also see it as bringing hope to a pool of wonderfully talented musicians.

I know from growing up and studying in Mexico City that there is such talent and desire in the musicians there. But there is also a belief that musicians have no hope of making it big in the world of classical music.

Now that I've had this wonderful opportunity to study in New York City and make these connections, I want this orchestra to provide an opportunity to young people in Central and South America—to give a chance to young composers and performers in these countries to come here and have a platform to showcase their talent.

I want the young people to think, "If I work hard, there is a way for me to do this." I also want them to believe that anything is possible, no matter what their age.

It's important to have a clear mission. If that is strong and you are willing to work hard, everything will come from that. Then say it to yourself as if your dream is already true. I did that when I had to find a sponsor for the orchestra. I introduced myself as "Alondra de la Parra, artistic director for the Philharmonic Orchestra of the Americas," even though the orchestra didn't truly exist yet. It didn't matter. The sponsors responded to my vision and came through.

I found there is no limit. Just keep going and don't stop. Watching your vision come true is the sweetest music of all.

You can learn more about the Philharmonic Orchestra of the Americas at poamericas.org.

Finding Your Magic

Jon Dorenbos,
NFL player, magician, and son of a murdered mother

I'm living the American sports dream, playing in the
NFL as a long snapper for the Philadelphia Eagles. I'm also a successful
magician, performing all over the country. But underneath my green
and white football helmet and my magic tricks lies a dark family history.
When I was 12 years old, my father killed my mother. This is my story:
how I used sports and magic to get through my tragic past and help
others along the way.

I make a living being a magician both on and off the field. On the
field I'm the long snapper for the Philadelphia Eagles. A long snapper is
a specialist who hikes the ball on punts, field goals, and extra points. If
you know football you know that this is an important but almost totally
invisible position. Most football fans don't even know that someone like
me exists, and then poof! The ball just appears in the hands of the punter
or at the foot of the kicker.

It's sort of a sleight of hand trick really—which is something
else I know quite a bit about. In my off hours I do magic shows and
demonstrations for corporations, nonprofit entities, and as a warm-up
act for major entertainers across the country.

I have had the chance to impact the lives of people in the corporate world and of countless children and adults stricken with cancer, illness, and heartache.

I know a little bit about heartache too.

I grew up in a northern suburb of Seattle called Woodinville. My dad was a hotshot executive at Microsoft and had just made the move over to an upstart company called Oracle Software. My mom was a pretty housewife, and my brother, sister, and I were all very close. I was the baby, and life appeared to be perfect.

But that was all about to come to an abrupt halt. When I was 12 I went to a baseball camp. I was a fairly good ballplayer and I was hoping to hone my skills and go big time some day. On my first day at camp, I was summoned by the sheriff to come down to the station. He said there had been an accident and I needed to come quickly.

The parents of some good friends went with me to the police station, where I found out my parents had had some sort of fight and that my mom "didn't make it." Apparently she had fallen down a staircase and hit her head. That's what the police told me anyway.

The truth was that my dad murdered my mother. He tried to cover it up, but the police weren't stupid, and his story quickly unraveled. He confessed to a grisly and cruel murder. By the time I was in sixth grade, my previously wonderful life had been totally erased.

My father ultimately turned himself in and confessed. I was asked to testify against him, which I did. He was convicted of second-degree murder. When I went to visit him in the state penitentiary, he would barely speak to me and told me I was no longer a part of his life. That was the last time I spoke to him.

After the trial I lived in the bedroom above the garage at the home of my foster parents, Kathy and Don Robson. On clear nights in Washington, you can see the Milky Way and millions of stars. There were stars that would stay still and there were stars that would move. It sounds kind of corny now, but I told myself I was headed toward the stars that stayed still. There was something out there that was worth going to. I knew my mom was guiding my journey, and I had the peace of knowing it would all work out all right.

My siblings and I moved in with my aunt Susan and her husband in Southern California. My grandparents lived close by, and we felt as though we'd landed someplace normal. After what we'd endured, it was a relief.

Because of what happened to me, I always felt older than other kids my age. My aunt called me "an old soul." I knew exactly what I wanted to do with my life and I was completely focused. (I never did any drugs at all and I never even touched alcohol until I was 22.) One way or another I was going to be a big-time ballplayer. Honestly I think I just wanted to make my mom proud.

Back in Washington I'd been on a good team, and my ex-coach invited me to come back to play in an all-star Little League baseball tournament. I stayed with the coach and his son. Their next-door neighbor was a man named Michael. Michael did magic. When I saw him doing some tricks, I thought magic was the coolest thing I'd ever seen. He took me to a local magic store and bought me my first book, called *Coin Magic*.

> Football and magic have given me the chance to meet so many people who have taught me more than I can ever repay them for.

I returned to California and practiced magic 24 hours a day for six years, night and day. I'd lie in bed at night practicing coin rolls and palming; then I'd look up and it would be 4 a.m. and I had school!

Naturally I got very good. I got so good in fact that I entered an eighth-grade talent show and did the David Copperfield trick of levitating an origami rose, then having it burst into flame and turn into a real rose. When I did the trick, there was complete silence in the room. I thought I'd done something wrong. Then the place erupted into wild applause. I won the contest.

By the time I graduated from high school, I was playing football more than baseball. I attended junior college but I wasn't as good a player as I'd hoped I would be. Then one day I received a call from my best friend, Paul Tessier, who played for The University of Texas, El Paso (UTEP), telling me that their long snapper had graduated. He asked if I could do that, and I said yes, even though I never had. In a fit of hubris, I sent them a video of our junior college snapper. UTEP saw the video and offered me a scholarship over the phone! (After my friend showed me how to do it, I snapped punts and field goals for UTEP for three years.)

On Pro Day, when the NFL scouts came to check out players, I had the best snapping day of my life, despite two hernias and two pulled groin tendons that required painkilling shots. I was in the zone. The scouts liked me, so I got an agent, Ken Harris, who totally believed in me and got my name around the NFL.

I made the team in Buffalo, New York. My first game was a scrimmage against the Cleveland Browns on August 2, 2004, exactly 11 years to the day my mom was killed.

My football career and magic career have been amazing. They've given me the chance to meet so many hurting people, who have in turn taught me more about life and living with passion than I can ever repay them for.

As for my dad, I don't know that I've forgiven him for taking my mom from me. I do know that sometimes people get so lost, and sometimes they just plain give up. I forgive him for that. That level of forgiveness allows me to wake up each morning and breathe in fresh air, like a burden is lifted. But I still miss my mom terribly.

I like to think my mom looks down on me and smiles. Today I play for the Philadelphia Eagles, loving my life and trying to bring magic to every life situation I encounter.

Although I play football in front of millions, my dream is to do magic in front of millions. That's my far-off star, but it's not that far away any more. I'll get there. If I've learned anything, it's that magic happens whenever you aim high and don't stop until you arrive.

For more on Jon Dorenbos, go to cal-entertainment.com.

Yosemite Facelift

Ken Yager,
rock climber and National Park cleanup organizer

It breaks my heart to see Yosemite National Park, one of the prettiest places on earth, littered with trash. So I decided to do something about it. Now once a year thousands of people I don't even know join me to clean up a piece of paradise. I call it "The Yosemite Facelift."

I fell in love with Yosemite the first time I ever saw the place, when I was 13 years old. My parents took our family there to go camping. On the way out of the park, I asked my parents to pull the car over and wait while I ran up to the base of El Capitan. For those of you who have never seen this magnificent piece of rock, it's 3,300 feet straight up—a giant chunk of granite that looks like the front of an ocean liner. I touched that massive rock and knew immediately that I wanted to climb it. That has been my life's passion ever since, climbing the rocks and mountains of Yosemite.

We have everything here: big walls, great crack climbing, super face climbing. There's good bouldering here as well, not to mention the amazing scenery. I've long made the area near Yosemite my home.

About 15 years ago I started seeing a lot of trash around the area. I'm not sure why visitors started respecting the place less, but I knew I'd seen a change. Near turnouts and alongside the roadways I started finding lots of toilet paper and baby diapers. In some cases there were even bags of trash that were just dumped. It's beyond me how people can treat such a beautiful place this way.

I tried picking up trash myself, but the job was too big. I would spend an hour or two at the job, only to find the area littered all over again two or three weeks later. Finally I got so fed up that I decided something had to change. I decided to organize a cleanup.

I am a rock-climbing guide by trade. For years visitors have hired me to guide them up the face of steep rock cliffs. Beyond throwing a good party or two, however, I knew absolutely nothing about organizing any kind of event. But in 2004 I decided to try something. I picked a cleanup date and then organized a gathering about two weeks ahead of time. On the day of the cleanup we had a pretty good turnout—a few more than 300 people showed up. Over three days we picked up about 5,000 to 6,000 pounds of trash.

People had such a positive attitude and were really gung ho. It was amazing how much we were able to accomplish. I couldn't believe the difference afterward just driving into the park—it looked clean!

Little did I know I was starting a tradition. Just by chance the date I picked that first year fell on National Public Lands Day. Someone at the permit office pointed that out to me. It's the day the National Environmental Education Foundation supports efforts to care for public and shared lands, and it means there are grants available to support and help organize efforts like the Yosemite Facelift. So now the Facelift takes place each year on National Public Lands Day.

People come to Yosemite for this cleanup from everywhere. We have climbers, school groups, families. In 2007 we even had one family come from Switzerland. They say they plan to come back every year because they had such a good time.

Apparently they aren't the only ones who enjoyed it because every year the event has doubled in size from the year before, both in the number of people who participate and in the amount of trash we pick up. In 2007 2,945 people came. Over five days we picked up 42,330 pounds of trash! We covered 132 miles of roadway and more than 80 miles of trails.

You wouldn't believe the things the volunteers hauled in: toilet paper, diapers, cigarette butts, beer cans—even odd things like an old pogo stick, foreign money, and a bottle with a purple-haired troll doll inside.

Three years ago we also started bringing in infrastructure that's been abandoned throughout the park, such as old telephone poles, power lines, and other things the Park Service doesn't have the funding to remove.

It might seem strange, but our volunteers really have a good time picking up all this trash. They come in holding bags of debris with big smiles on their faces. It feels good to do a big project with a lot of people. I've also gotten sponsors to donate prizes and we have daily raffles. In the evenings I organize a movie or slide show.

> Tackling a big project is like climbing El Capitan: Just focus on what's right in front of you and take it one section at a time.

This has also been good for what can be a strained relationship between climbers and the Park Service. The tension comes from park rules that limit how long visitors can camp inside the park. Stays are limited to a couple of weeks during the summer to allow more visitors to cycle through.

For climbers those restrictions are tough to follow. The rocks here are hard, slippery, and scary, and it takes time to start feeling comfortable with them. A couple of weeks is not enough, so a lot of climbers camp in out-of-bounds areas for a month or two. This pits the climbers against the park rangers, who have to enforce the rules. I can see both sides.

The good news is this cleanup brings both sides together. In 2007 the Park Service put a value of $344,188 on all the cleanup work. In turn, the Park Service has given us a booth outside the visitors center during the cleanup and sets aside some campsites for Facelift volunteers.

I honestly never thought I would be the one to organize something so big. Frankly I'm doing it because no one else is. If someone else had stepped up, I would be saying, "Great! I'm going climbing!"

If you are frustrated by the state of your surroundings, I would say the only way you are going to change things is by doing rather than complaining. We need to teach by example. You can't complain about someone else unless you start with yourself. Clean up the area that offends you. You'll feel good that it got done and you'll find your actions are contagious. I had one dad email me, writing, "After we got back from Yosemite, my son and his friend felt inspired to clean up a park in San Francisco. Now they're organizing a cleanup for their school." That kind of feedback makes me feel really good.

If the thought of cleaning up someone else's mess seems offensive, consider that we've all littered sometime, even if unintentionally.

And don't let lack of know-how stop you. I knew nothing about organizing thousands of volunteers for such a big project, but it turned out to be a lot like climbing my beloved El Capitan. If you stand at the base and look up, it's overwhelming. But if you break it down and just focus on what's right in front of you, you can tackle that section and then the next and the next.

That's how I've tackled every project I've ever done. And just as in making my way up a giant rock, I often come to a point where I thought I was going to go one way, but that direction isn't open. So I look around to find another route. It's always obvious when the time comes.

When I reached the boiling point on all the litter around Yosemite, I couldn't see at first how it was all going to get picked up. Now I do—with the help of 2,945 of my new friends. That is, until next year when I'll probably have twice as many.

You can learn more about The Yosemite Facelift at yosemiteclimbing.org.

Daryn's Takeaways

. . . .

You won't see me hanging off a rock face anytime soon, but I am going to hang on to Ken's analogy of breaking down the task of climbing an imposing mountain. It really is just one step at a time, isn't it? Staying focused on the task right in front of you means truly being in the present, breaking big jobs down into doable tasks.

What about you? Do you have a dream to better the world that seems bigger than your experience prepares you to handle? How can you scale it down to a level that feels more manageable? How could you improve your world?

Part 4

··

Giving Back: Ordinary People, Extraordinary Humanitarians

A Hospital for Harar

Sebri Omer,
Ethiopian immigrant, gas station owner,
and hospital founder

I have learned many things since I came to the
United States 25 years ago. I know you don't have to wait until you're
a billionaire to get things done and make a difference in the world.
Thinking you have no money is no excuse. I'm living proof: I managed to
build a hospital back in the country I was forced to flee as a teenager.

I was born 47 years ago in the war-torn city of Harar, Ethiopia. By the
time I was 17, it was clear to my parents that it was far too dangerous for
a young man to stay in Ethiopia. The government was targeting young
people, believing they were part of an overthrow movement. To stay
would mean certain death.

Even though I had never traveled anywhere else and knew not a
soul in the world outside my hometown, I fled on foot, walking across
Ethiopia to the neighboring country of Djibouti. It took seven weeks to
get there only to find more challenges. There wasn't much food. Some
days I only drank water. There were many refugees trying to figure out
what their next step would be.

After two years in Djibouti, my luck turned around, thanks to a
program run by the United Nations. The UN was assigning refugees to

different countries that were willing to take them in. I could have landed in any number of places in the world. Somehow I was sent to what I believe is the greatest country in the world, the United States.

I arrived in Philadelphia and immediately enrolled in high school. I wanted to make up for the time I had lost in my education. I completed high school in two years and went on to study marketing in college. This country amazes me. If you want to go to school, there are schools. You want to work hard? There are jobs. I've sometimes worked three jobs at a time simply because the opportunity was there.

My American Dream led me to Georgia. I married, started my family and my own business, eventually buying two gas station convenience stores and a car wash. This didn't happen overnight, of course. But before I knew it, 20 years had passed since I had left Ethiopia.

> It seemed natural to call the hospital Yemage. That is my son's name, and it also means "hope" in my native language.

About this time, things had calmed down some in the area around my hometown of Harar. In fact, a new government was in charge and encouraging emigrants to come back, visit, and perhaps invest in a growing economy. I thought this was a wonderful opportunity to go home, see family, and perhaps invest in a business such as building a hotel.

My plans changed as soon as I arrived in Harar. I received word that a dear relative was in the hospital, so I went to visit him. I was shocked by what I saw. There were more than 20 patients in a single room, each with different illnesses. Tiles were hanging from the ceiling, ready to fall on the patients. The sheets were dirty. The needles were rusty.

It was nothing like the conditions I've come to expect in American hospitals where sheets are changed, the floor is spotless, the water is clean, and there is modern medical equipment.

Right there, visiting my relative, the inspiration came to me. Forget the hotel, I would build a hospital in my hometown! It might have only two or three beds, but it would be clean and it would have trained staff and the best equipment available.

To many people this might have seemed like an unrealistic dream.

There is no such facility in all of Ethiopia. As far as money, all my savings were invested in my businesses back in America. But I didn't waste any time getting started.

I contacted government officials, who very much liked my idea. In fact, they gave me a 60-acre plot of land. I picked a cluster of buildings that were in a good location but had been bombed out and abandoned during the war. Still, there was the challenge of finding the funds to rebuild those buildings.

I was able to get one loan from an Ethiopian bank, and then it came time to do my part. When I returned to America, I sat down with my family and presented my plan: to sell half of our businesses. I did the math and showed them we could survive fine with just one gas station. I explained, "We can still eat and we can still drive. But what about the people back in Ethiopia?" My family was very supportive and agreed, so we sold the second gas station and car wash. The $40,000 profit was the final piece I needed.

In 2001 the Yemage Medical Center opened. It had 25 beds to start. We are now up to 45 beds. We do in- and outpatient care. Thanks to a recent donation, we now have the only working ambulance in all of Ethiopia. We do surgery and obstetrics/gynecology. We have an X-ray machine and we also have an in-house pharmacy. Many of the supplies have come from a wonderful organization, MedShare International.

We have a full-time staff running the hospital, including a doctor and nurses. I visit twice a year to make sure everything is running up to standards. These visits are so joyful for me. I watch people who are extremely sick get the help they need, then walk out of the hospital. That experience is an unbelievable enjoyment that you cannot buy.

It seemed natural to call the hospital Yemage. That happens to be my son's name. It also means "hope" in my native language. We are hoping the facility will bring hope to the citizens of Harar for many years to come.

As for my own hopes, I've already set my next dream in motion. I want to build an HIV/AIDS hospice right next to the medical center. AIDS has become a terrible problem in Ethiopia. There isn't a single hospice in the entire country. I dream of a 175-bed center where AIDS patients can find kind and proper care and support for their families.

I already have the land and the site plans for the hospice. Now comes the matter of raising the funds. I'm told it will take more than $100,000 to build the kind of facility I believe the people of Harar need. I have no more gas stations or car washes I can sell off to finance this part, so to some people it might appear that I'm stuck.

Well, some people tried to tell me building the hospital was too big a dream. But if you concentrate and focus, anything's possible, and I have formed a nonprofit organization to raise the funds.

Because of my success, I encourage others to make a difference in the world as well. You can wait to be a billionaire and build a 2,000-bed hospital. Or you can build a one-bed hospital with only a few thousand dollars. And do it now. The point is to help people.

As for the sacrifice I made in selling half the businesses I worked so hard to build, I don't miss them one bit. Sure, they would today be bringing me more American dollars. But that money couldn't bring me an ounce of the joy I get by helping heal my African hometown.

You can learn more about the hospital at yemagemedicalcenter.com.

Daryn's Takeaways

. . . .

I love how Sebri lives in a world of opportunity. He saw an opportunity to work hard and build a business when he came to the United States. And he saw an opportunity to give back long before most people would think they were able to do so. Sure, he made a big sacrifice in selling half his businesses to finance the hospital in Ethiopia. Even if we're not ready to take that kind of step, we can all learn from Sebri's spirit of doing what we can right now with what we have. Why wait?

What dreams of making a difference in the world are you putting off because you don't think you have enough money? If you lowered the scale of what you wished to create, what could you do right now?

Fulfilling Children's Dreams

Henri Landwirth,
Holocaust survivor and founder of Give Kids the World

I wear the number B4343 tattooed on the inside of my left forearm. It is a reminder of how the Nazis stole my family and my childhood. More than 67 years later, I have prospered in this great country, America. I use my good fortune to create a happy place for sick children who also are at risk of losing the carefree days of their childhood.

I believe I am living on borrowed time. There is no explanation of how I survived five years in Nazi death camps. But I can explain how I chose to abandon hate and why I vow to make the most of every moment and every day.

In 1939 I was 13 years old, living in Krakow, Poland, with my parents and twin sister, Margot, when the Nazis came for us. We were like so many Jewish families who didn't see the extreme danger coming. Actually my father feared the Nazis, but my mother wanted to stay in Poland and was convinced that it was safe to do so.

We all learned a very different reality when the Nazis came and took my father away later that year. They put him in prison without a trial. I later learned he was massacred with several other men just outside the prison. Each man was shot in the back of the head with a rifle. The bodies were dumped in an unmarked mass grave.

My mother, sister, and I were forced to go to a series of concentration camps. Like many families we were separated. The next four years were a blur of horrendous conditions, different camps, and hunger and suffering beyond words.

Yet somehow I survived.

As the war came to a close, an incident happened that I thought surely was the end of my young life. A group of Nazi soldiers marched four other prisoners and me into the woods to shoot us. For some reason they had a change of heart. Instead of aiming their guns at us, they shot into the air and allowed us to flee.

I made my way through a series of relocation centers in Poland and Germany and learned my mother was killed just weeks before the war ended. I was devastated and all the more determined to find my sister.

Somehow I made it to a small town in the middle of Germany where I had heard some young women survivors were staying. That's where I experienced the miracle of being reunited with Margot. That day remains one of the happiest ever in my life.

We both made it to the United States, and I began to make the most of my borrowed time. As I see it, I was as good as dead that day in the woods with those Nazi soldiers. Every day since is a bonus.

Not too long after I arrived in the United States with only $20 in my pocket, I received a letter from the president. I thought it was a welcome letter. It turned out to be a draft notice. This was incredible since I didn't even speak English yet. Still I went and fulfilled my military service.

> I was as good as dead that day in the woods with those Nazi soldiers. Every day since is a bonus.

When I completed my service, I was able to go to college on the GI Bill, and I chose to study hotel management.

I started from the bottom up at a couple of hotels in New York City. Then in 1954 I moved to Florida. The Sunshine State truly turned out to be the land of great opportunity for me. I managed the Starlite Motel in Cocoa Beach, near Cape Canaveral. I made lifelong friendships with all the astronauts who stayed there over the years.

The hotel business was good to me as I went from manager to owner.

This was about the time a man named Walt Disney came to central Florida looking to develop Disney World. Building hotels to support this booming resort area proved to be incredibly lucrative.

Yet even as I was making more money than I could ever imagine, I knew that all the hotels and all the money in the world could not make me happy. Then I discovered a wonderful passion: the passion of giving.

First I started a foundation with some of the astronauts. The Mercury Seven Foundation is now called the Astronaut Scholarship Foundation. Since the beginning it has provided scholarships for science students.

Next I founded the Fanny Landwirth Foundation in honor of my dear mother. The foundation has built a school and senior citizen center in Orlando and continues to fund many other charities around the world.

Then in 1986 I heard about a little girl named Amy who had terminal cancer. Her family had been planning a trip to Disney World to make Amy's final wish come true. She wanted to meet Mickey Mouse.

I heard from one of my hotel managers that Amy's family canceled the trip because she died before they could make it happen. This absolutely broke my heart. How could this happen? This is such a great country. How could a dying child's wish not be granted?

I vowed this would never happen again. That was the beginning of Give Kids the World (GKTW).

Today GKTW is a village in Kissimmee, Florida, right next to Orlando. My staff and I cut through all the red tape and practically overnight make a child's dream of visiting Disney World and the theme parks come true.

The entire family is flown to Florida and put up at GKTW's whimsical village. The family receives tickets to all the attractions, meals, and rental car at no cost to them.

We're able to make all this possible thanks to the great relationships I have developed through my hotel company with Florida vendors over the years. The theme parks are happy to work with GKTW because they know their free tickets are going to deserving families.

GKTW has hosted more than 75,000 families from all 50 states and more than 50 countries.

I simply love hosting these children. I see myself in them and I understand what they are going through. They face disease, and I faced the Nazis. They feel like they have no control over their lives, just like I had no control over mine. We are all survivors and fighters with a will to live. I get such joy knowing I can do something about making their wish come true.

I have done incredible things with my life after surviving the Holocaust. I came to America where I made my fortune, I have three beloved children, and I have given away a lot of money.

> I have done incredible things with my life after surviving the Holocaust. But the most important thing was to let go of hate.

But the most important thing I did for myself was to let go of the hate. There are no words for how much I hated the Germans after the war, and I think anyone would say I had good reason. But I gradually made an observation: Despising them, hating them, and doing evil to them simply made me like they were. The last thing I wanted to be was them.

It's terrible to live with hate. Hate hurts. There is no value for the person who holds on to hate. It is possible, though, to take that same effort of hating and turn it into love and caring. That's how I found my way to a happy and fulfilling life.

I know it's hard for some people to understand. My own sister has never forgiven the Nazis for all that they did to our family. But for me, I have had a much better life by spending my time giving.

GKTW presents an opportunity for many others to give as well. The village operates thanks to a roster of 5,000 volunteers. Many of them are senior citizens who never want to leave the village. They find, like me, that by giving, each day is a miracle.

You can learn more at GiveKidsTheWorld.com and HateHurts.org.

Daryn's Takeaways

Henri Landwirth seems remarkable because he gave up hating the very people who destroyed his family. How could any human forgive such terrible acts? Yet if you read carefully, you'll realize that Henri sees giving up hate as a gift to himself, not to those who harmed him and his family.

By giving up hate, he freed himself to love. Just look at the joy he experiences creating amazing childhood memories for the kids who come to his village. I don't imagine he would have the capacity to experience such joy if he were consumed by hate. It's a great lesson.

How much of your day do you spend harboring bad feelings for someone who has harmed you? Whom are you really hurting with those feelings? What do you lose if you let them go? What joy awaits you if you release them?

Cartridges for a Cure ®

Eli Kahn,
childhood cancer survivor and teen recycler

The biggest obstacle of my life started before I can even remember. I was diagnosed with leukemia when I was only 2½. Not only did I beat that potentially deadly disease, I've come up with a creative way to give back to the doctors who saved my life and to help the environment at the same time.

I'm 16 years old, and I'm here to tell you that kids can make a difference. My life has been different in many ways since I was a baby and diagnosed with leukemia.

If you don't know, leukemia is cancer of the bone marrow and blood. Basically there's an uncontrollable accumulation of and damage to the white blood cells in your body. Anemia and lack of disease-fighting white blood cells leave you wide open to various infections. Anybody can get leukemia at any time, and doctors don't know what causes it. All they know is that it kills you. But doctors told my parents that if my treatment went as expected, I had more than an 80 percent chance of survival.

My doctors at Johns Hopkins Hospital in Baltimore were the best. My pediatrician sent us there over Christmas break in 1993 when I had a strange fever that would not go away. Of course, I was too young to remember much, but my parents tell me the situation was very serious.

I immediately underwent chemotherapy. Then I had to spend every other weekend for six months at the Johns Hopkins Children's Center, followed by another two years of outpatient chemotherapy, which included having blood drawn through an infusaport implanted in my chest.

Ten years later I'm cancer-free and considered to be in 100 percent remission.

A complete recovery from leukemia is amazing. But my story doesn't stop there. It really started when I turned 12 and was studying for my bar mitzvah. Part of the preparation meant I had to complete a community service project. Since my cancer treatment and recovery were such a big part of my life, I wanted to do something to help out Johns Hopkins Hospital. I felt the need to give back to those people who literally gave me back my life.

But what could a kid do to help out a cancer center?

I went online and found that one of the simplest money-making ideas out there was recycling printer cartridges. Sounds simple, right? It was and still is. But the results have amazed everyone, including me.

At first only family and friends knew about my project, but as it grew I set up a website with instructions and a form for people to fill out for mailing information and free postage supplies. The website notifies me that someone needs the mailing supplies. I notify the recycling company, and it sends the mailing supplies directly to the customer, who then packages the used ink cartridges and returns them to the company for recycling.

I don't handle the cartridges, except for the few that people drop by my house. I make about a dollar a cartridge, and the California-based recycling company sends me a check each time it receives a submission of cartridges.

Things started out slowly. At first I was receiving checks for $15 or $20 each month. My original goal had been to raise $1,800. In Judaism 18 is considered a lucky number, so I thought that $1,800 in contributions would be a good target to shoot for. But at $15 or $20 a month, it would take forever. I thought there had to be a better way.

I did more research and discovered the company I was working with was just a middleman. It was taking a huge cut for basically doing nothing. I learned I could become a rep for the main company and keep a much larger piece of the action. So that's what I did.

And things took off from there! The program's monthly income immediately jumped to $500 to $1,000 a month! I couldn't believe it. Apparently other people were amazed as well, because I started getting some media coverage. That brought even more business! I sent all the money to Johns Hopkins, making the hospital very happy.

A lot of leukemia research is done on zebra fish because their bone marrow and blood cell production is similar to that of humans. The money I raise is used to buy fish tanks and more fish or whatever else they need. As it turns out, the doctor that treated me is one of the leading researchers in the nation.

> I had no idea how hungry the world is for people to take action, and when you do, amazing things start to happen.

This has all grown way past my original bar mitzvah service project. As a result of all the exposure, I was nominated for the Lands' End "Born Heroes" award. Out of thousands of entrants, I made it to the final three and was awarded $5,000—which I turned over to the folks at Johns Hopkins Hospital. Then I was nominated for the Volvo for Life award and donated that $50,000 as well. So far I've sent the hospital more than $85,000.

And all this works with hardly any effort on my part. Honestly I'm just a normal high school kid who plays water polo and golf, likes music, and hangs out with my friends. Someday I'd like to be a sports agent. I'm as normal as can be. But I set up this simple system that just churns out money for a great cause.

My whole family is involved too. My sister has started a campuswide recycling project at Syracuse University and has done fundraisers for Johns Hopkins Hospital. My parents have served on several of the hospital's boards and committees. I'm amazed at how much good can come from one simple action, like setting up a recycling outfit for a bar mitzvah project.

I'm often asked how I'd suggest other young people raise money for charity. I always suggest that they find something that's easy to do and that they feel personally connected to. It might be starving kids they see on TV, a homeless shelter they care about, or an animal rescue center.

You don't have to be an organization to do something good for an organization or a cause. Just get started. Find something that excites you.

And get ready. I had no idea how hungry the world is for people to take action, and when you do, amazing things start to happen. Try it and see for yourself. I'm still young, and thanks to the doctors at Johns Hopkins Hospital, I have a lot of living to do. But this experience has changed everything for me and will shape me, and many others, for years to come.

For more information visit CartridgesForACure.com.

The Million-Dollar Resale Shop

Marie Hesser,
cofounder of a charitable resale shop

It feels great to make $1 million with the express
purpose of giving most of it away. I know because I'm one in a group of
ladies from Stillwater, Oklahoma, who did just that, even though at the
beginning we knew very little about making money.

This is a story of what you can do when you decide you can. In the
fall of 2001, we were a group of 30 women ranging in age from the mid-
thirties to the mid-eighties with a passion to make an impact on our town
of 40,000.

We decided to open our own resale shop. That might not have
sounded like the best idea at the time since Stillwater already had four
resale shops. But none were like the one we envisioned. We wanted
it to be unique and to carry beautiful items. We wanted it to be clean,
spacious, and bright. We decided to call it Elite Repeat.

That's all we had at the beginning: the idea, the inspiration, and the
agreement that none of us would be paid a single cent. Yes, we all agreed
to be volunteers and give all our profits away. Our original group came
from all walks of life: nurses, teachers, homemakers, dental assistants,

farmers' wives. That diversity served us well because one person might be good at appraising antiques, another at design and display.

I laugh now because the only thing we didn't have at the beginning was someone who thought she was good with money. You would think that would be important in running a shop. But we didn't care because we thought we could do it anyway. I agreed to be the bookkeeper only because no one else wanted the job. I knew nothing—*nothing!*—about bookkeeping. But we just proceeded as if everything would work out.

As a group we decided our money would go to two charities: Habitat for Humanity and our local Community Action Agency, which provides services for the homeless and a medical clinic for the poor. Our research showed that both organizations had good structures and goals but were short on cash. That's where we came in.

I smile when I think back to my first visit to the local Habitat for Humanity board. When I told them we were opening this shop and wanted them to be one of our primary beneficiaries, they looked at me as if to say, "Well, that's nice"—as if we were some cute old ladies who were having a bake sale. Let's just say they don't look at us like that anymore.

Even though they didn't expect much money from us, the Habitat folks helped us fix up our first downtown store location. We bought the supplies, and they did the painting and construction. One of those Habitat volunteers was a retired accountant. He became our accountant and business manager, and he has been a true gift. I was more than happy to turn over the two pages of ledger work I had done up to that point.

Of course, we needed something to sell. Some of us fanned out to local garage sales. If we liked what we saw, we would leave behind a flyer saying we would love to have their leftovers. We didn't have to do that for very long. News about our shop spread quickly by word of mouth. Now folks say, "Take it down to Elite Repeat." They know we take good care of things, and the money we raise stays in Stillwater and surrounding communities.

Speaking of money, we needed a little seed money to get started for things like paint, clothing racks, and other supplies. Two of us put in a total of $10,000. Every cent was paid back to us with interest within three months!

It was evident that the shop was going to be a success from the very beginning. The rent for our first shop was $1,300 a month. Our very first day we made $1,760, which of course covered our rent and then some. We just kept going from there.

We've now given Habitat for Humanity more than $200,000. We even funded the building of one of their houses entirely by ourselves. They call it The Elite Repeat House. The Habitat folks helped out again when it was time to move. Yes, this shop, started by a group of ladies who knew nothing about running a store or a nonprofit organization, has now doubled in size. We moved across the street to a storefront with 7,000 square feet.

Our volunteer list now numbers 65. How do you attract and motivate people to work for no money? Good communication and inclusion. Volunteers who work at the store sit on our board of directors, and we listen to their input on how best to run the shop.

> We didn't have a business plan, only a belief plan, a belief that we could do this and everything we needed would show up.

There have been challenges as we figured out how to do this. Some people had to become the managers. Five of us each took a day and made decisions that day. That plan worked out well until one of the managers moved away, one started having grandbabies and began caring for them, and one manager's husband retired and wanted her home more with him. We just let the process evolve. Now we have coordinators who can open, close, and collect money.

Our shop has made over $1 million, and we've given away $700,000. The rest of the money goes for things like rent, supplies, utilities, and snacks. (Coffee breaks and fellowship are important to us.) We've done so well that we added a third charity recipient, Domestic Violence Services.

Even with the extra recipient, however, we found ourselves at the end of 2006 with an extra $30,000. So we gave it to our Stillwater YMCA and three other charities.

You might think we would have problems with the four other resale shops in Stillwater, but it's never been said that we took away anyone else's business. It's more like we created business where there was none. We garnered goodwill by sending customers to other shops if they were looking for something we didn't have.

Our message to others is that if we can be successful in Stillwater, Oklahoma, a town of 40,000 with four other resale shops, then anyone can. We didn't have a business plan, only a belief plan, a belief that we could do this and everything we needed would show up. We never thought about what was going to stop us. We only thought about all the help that kept showing up—like our business manager, the volunteers from Habitat for Humanity, and the paying customers and donors who come every day.

And they do keep coming. With an average of 90 paying customers daily, we now generate about $19,000 in sales a month, which enables us to give away $15,000 every month. It's clear that Elite Repeat has taken on a life of its own and will be here benefiting Stillwater long after all of us are gone.

You can see more about the shop at eliterepeat.org.

Daryn's Takeaways

* *

The women who created The Elite Repeat shop might not have started with what looked like the smartest business plan, but they had something that I think was just as important, a belief plan. They began with the simple belief that they could succeed. They also had a clear vision of what they wanted to create and why. I know that creating a belief plan was some of the best advice I received as I was launching my own business. Write down the answers to these simple questions:

Why are you in business?

What values are important to you?

What are your nonnegotiable values about your work, your time, and the impact on your family?

Your answers will help you create a template for your business whether you're the boss, an employee, or a volunteer. Create your employment with intention; it will be much easier to decide with whom you work and why.

Changing Gang Mentality

Ernesto Luis Romero,
cofounder Homies Unidos

I am the last man you would want to support

and give money. That's if you look at my past. You'll see a guy who was
a drug addict and gang member and went to jail 36 times. But let me
show you what I've been doing since 1992. You'll see how I've cleaned up,
left the gang life, and am now helping thousands of other gang members
do the same.

I understand why boys and young men join gangs: They want a place
to belong. I know that was the case with me.

I grew up in San Salvador, El Salvador, in the 1980s. When I was 14,
civil war was raging all around my country. Boys my age ended up in the
army or fighting with the guerillas. My mother didn't want either of those
for me, so she sent me to live with relatives in California.

That meant taking what little money my family had to send me over
the border illegally. They hired what's called a coyote, someone who
smuggles illegals into the United States in the back of a car or a truck.
For me that meant being stuffed into the trunk of an old Cadillac with
10 other people!

Once we made it into California, I found my way to relatives just
outside of Los Angeles in El Cerito. They were so happy to see me that

they threw a party. We ate chicken and pork chops and all these different foods that I had never tried before.

The happy times quickly came to an end. My relatives and I had very different ideas about what I should be doing now that I was in the United States. I wanted to go to school, to finish high school, and then maybe go on to something else. But my family told me, "No. You must find a job." They were all hard workers and believed I should do the same: contribute to their household and send money back home.

My uncle got me a job with a mechanic. The man taught me how to work on transmissions. He fed me. He paid me $1 a day. He also introduced me to drugs.

That's where I started smoking weed and snorting cocaine. Before I knew it I was spending all my money on drugs. My California relatives grew tired of me quickly. "What happened with your job?" they wanted to know. "You don't bring any money home. You're stoned all the time."

When I started stealing from my aunts to get more money for drugs, they kicked me out. I was 15 years old, living on the streets of Los Angeles.

I found a job parking cars, and the guy who took the money for the tickets soon taught me another skill: how to deal drugs. He explained, "If you sell this little $7 bag for $10, then you're going to earn $3. The extra is for you."

That sent me on a five-year spiral into more drugs and more addiction. I felt so alone until I found this group of people who said they wanted to help me. They gave me clothes, meals, showers. They even got me a haircut. I guess it's not surprising that I started hanging with them. I joined their gang.

They felt like my friends and family. I had to help them, even if that meant doing robberies. That's how I started going to jail. Thirty-six jail visits later I started getting the message.

Jail was actually a good thing for me. When I was in jail, I wasn't doing drugs. I also finally had the chance to get some of the education I wanted when I first came to the United States. I earned my GED.

My first daughter also helped me change my life. I loved her so much that I wanted to clean up my act for her.

This was about 1992, and peace had finally come to El Salvador. I knew it was time to go home.

Coming back to San Salvador, I saw the same gang problems as in the United States, only worse. So many of the young people grew up in unstable family environments because of the war. Unemployment was almost 50 percent, and the gangs gave lost young men a place to belong. But by now I understood that there was a better way.

Instead of doing drugs and alcohol, I started making projects for kids to give them an alternative to drugs and gangs. In 1996 I got a bunch of rival gang members to sit down and help form Homies Unidos. That means "Homies United." The young people can belong to something positive that can give value to their life. Sixteen other former gang members work with me in San Salvador. We also have people working back in California.

> Most of these kids are so used to violence—it's all they see—and they can't imagine a different world.

It's not easy getting through to young people. Many don't see any other way of life because their homes are shattered. The gangs, as bad as they are, are the only stability these young people know. Many aren't scared of anything, so they don't think twice about using intravenous drugs, getting tattoos with dirty needles, and having unprotected sex.

Our efforts to break through to these hardcore gangsters means being around them constantly, communicating, and never giving up. Most of these kids are so used to violence—it's all they see—and they can't imagine a different world. We encourage them to see that the violence they experience on a daily basis isn't the way life always has to be and that they can create a different kind of safety net for themselves.

For those who decide to come out of the gangs, Homies Unidos offers them good options. In places like El Salvador and Los Angeles, these kids face a lot of discrimination. No one wants to hire someone who shaves his head and has a bunch of tattoos. So we show them other ways to empower themselves. For example, we offer the Epiphany Program. This is a 10-week life skills program where we teach young people job and communication skills as well as how to apply for jobs and so on. This class also gives them new options for dealing with domestic violence and the criminal activity that goes on around them.

We also offer tattoo removal. Tattoos are a major part of gang members' identity, and when they decide to move their life upward, old tattoos can be a problem. If gang members agree to go through the Epiphany Program, we will help them get their tattoos removed. This is like a snake shedding its skin; self-esteem increases immediately and helps the young people take a step in the direction of a better life.

The Epiphany Program also teaches them business skills so they can open their own small business if they wish. That might, for example, mean teaching them how to bake so they can open their own bakeries.

This program has been very effective. We've helped more than 5,000 gang members, giving them drug rehab, education, and job training. More than 1,200 have learned enough to leave the gang life.

But sometimes gang members just don't want to leave. We don't give up on these kids. Instead we encourage them to look in the mirror and be honest with themselves: Is this the life they really want? We tell them to be very honest with themselves because they know exactly what the consequences are of staying in the gang. They aren't stupid. We just encourage them to be honest.

For the family members of kids in gangs, we also offer support. We encourage them to be involved with their kids' lives as much as possible and to listen to them, even if they don't agree with the choices the kids are making. We urge families to try to put themselves in their kids' shoes and win them back instead of judging, brutalizing, or attacking them. This sort of "strict and loving" approach builds trust over time.

Most gangs are about taking lives. We are about saving lives. We face a constant barrage of obstacles in accomplishing this, but it has to happen. Someone has to step up, and Homies Unidos is doing that.

For more information go to homiesunidos.org.

Compassion in Action

Zainab Salbi,
daughter of Saddam Hussein's private pilot,
social entrepreneur, and founder of
Women for Women International

As strange as it seems, my father was Saddam Hussein's private pilot. My family's dangerous connection to Saddam meant that I had to flee my country into an abusive arranged marriage just to save my life. I couldn't know at the time that this strange family life was preparing me for a career helping hundreds of thousands of women war refugees around the world.

My passion is helping women war refugees rebuild their lives. I come to this work naturally because of my own story.

When I was growing up in Baghdad, my father worked as Saddam's private pilot. But that meant so much more than just his job. The assignment came with a package. It meant our entire family had the social obligation to do whatever Saddam wanted. If he wanted us at a social function, we were there. When Saddam smiled, we smiled. When he laughed, we laughed.

I didn't know it at the time, but as I grew into a young woman, Saddam also had his eye on me. The situation set in motion a series of devastating and confusing events that I didn't understand until later.

My mother had raised me to be an independent woman. She always told me I should marry for love. She said, "No man should expect you to know how to clean just because you are a woman."

Suddenly, however, when I was about 20, she became adamant that I accept an arranged marriage proposal to a man I did not know who was living in the United States. She insisted I had to leave Iraq. Ten years later on her deathbed, she explained she was trying anything to get me out of the country and out of Saddam's reach.

Even though I dreaded the idea of marrying him and was confused about why my mother was begging me to accept, I was a dutiful daughter. I agreed to the marriage and came to Chicago.

The marriage was instantly horrible. My new husband did every terrible thing to me my mother had raised me never to accept. He was emotionally, physically, and verbally abusive, and raped me one time.

I knew enough to get out. I left with $400 in my purse, two suitcases of nice clothes, and nowhere to go. There was no going back to Iraq. My father had finally left Saddam's service, my parents divorced, and my family was being economically punished. On top of that, Saddam had invaded Kuwait. The first Gulf War was on. Going home was not an option because of the embargo and sanctions on the country.

I made my way to Los Angeles, then Washington, D.C., and started my life from scratch. I got a job and met the man who became my second husband. I was all of 23 years old.

One day I read a *Time* magazine article about horrendous rape camps in Bosnia. It described how women were herded into these camps simply to be gang-raped by soldiers. I don't think I could have pointed out Bosnia on a map, but I felt compelled to do something.

I thumbed through the phone book looking for women's organizations. Yes, the phone book since this was before everyone was using the Internet. Not a single group seemed to feel the same urgency about the Bosnian situation that I did. "We're going to monitor it for six months," one group told me.

"Six months?" I couldn't believe what I was hearing. "There are rape camps going on. We need to do something now." My idea was to do something as small as sponsor a single woman. I wanted to give her cash to have the freedom to do what she wanted to with the money. Let her

buy whatever she needed: food, clothes.

That's when I was connected to the Unitarian Church in Washington, D.C. I dressed up in a suit, borrowed my father-in-law's briefcase so that I would look official, and made my pitch in front of the board of directors. They agreed to help me for one year. During that time I was to figure out how to register as a nonprofit organization because after the year I was on my own.

My husband and I threw a fundraiser and added those funds to the money we had been saving to take a belated honeymoon to Spain. Instead of Spain, we headed to Croatia to start the program.

I immediately met the kind of woman I had hoped to help. Aysha had been held in the rape camp for nine months. They let her go only because she was eight months pregnant. She ended up losing that baby because of health complications.

The women I met in those rape camps changed my life forever. I came back and quit my job. My husband quit his doctoral study track to get a job to support us. Women for Women International was born.

Today, 14 years later, Women for Women has helped 120,000 women like Aysha. My staff and I have distributed $39 million in aid and loans. At this time we're working with 35,000 women survivors of wars.

> Despite the horrible things they've been through, these women still find joy.

Each of those women goes through a three-part program. First she is matched with a sponsor who provides her with a small amount of money to help her catch her breath. It allows her to eat, send her kids to school, and take care of the essentials while she gets her bearings.

We make it possible for each sponsor to write letters to the woman she is sponsoring. This is very important because it restores the women's faith in humanity. War has shown them the terrible things people can do to each other. But the letters shine the light on the best in humanity. They show that someone cares.

Then we help each woman rebuild her community support network. A group of 20 women goes through training together to learn vocational skills and to bond with and support fellow women refugees.

Finally each woman learns to move from victim to survivor to active citizen. She learns to say, "I'm going to take the lead in changing my life and my family." For some it's as simple as making changes within their own families, telling their husbands, "No, you will not beat me anymore." Some seek changes within their villages. Each one is different. The point is to help each woman take ownership of changing her life.

Women for Women International takes help beyond humanitarian aid. The aid is an important first step. But it's just as important to restore dignity to these women, help them get jobs, and heal their families.

This work has been absolutely incredible. I wake up each day and live by the motto "It's a good day to fly; it's a good day to die."

These women teach me how to fly. I've learned from them about joy in life. Yes, joy. Despite the horrible things they have been through, they still find moments to laugh, to sing, to dance.

Their resiliency inspires me to ask myself, "If they can smile, who am I not to smile? If they can sing, who am I not to sing?"

The satisfaction I get from this work also means each day I can say, "It's a good day to die." Going from war zone to war zone, I see that life and death coexist in the same moment. Because of this work I can say if I die today I will be content and fulfilled. I've made sure that I'm on a clean page with everyone in my life.

People tell me that I'm so lucky because I've done so much. It's always come with the price of taking a very big risk. There have been physical, emotional, and relationship risks.

It takes courage to take those leaps—courage that I learn from these women of war. I went into this work thinking I was going to save them. The truth is, these women have saved me.

You can learn more about Zainab Salbi at womenforwomen.org.

Daryn's Takeaways

I already knew Zainab was doing amazing work around the world. Interviewing her gave me a new standard for living each day: "A good day to fly; a good day to die."

It seems such a tall order, but is there any other way to live? We really only have today, this moment. Why not make the most of it and soar? And yes, why not be at peace with everyone in our lives?

Are you flying today? Have you made peace with everyone in your life?

Frozen Inspiration

Jill Youse,
mother and founder of International Breast Milk Project

Inspiration comes from the strangest places.

I found mine while staring at seemingly endless pouches of breast milk stored in my freezer. They were there for my baby daughter, Stella. Frankly I was producing more milk than a dairy. "I could feed half the babies in Africa," I thought in my punchy, sleep-deprived state. That's all I had in my bag of tricks to launch the International Breast Milk Project.

Before you go comparing me to Mother Teresa or something, let me explain: I was a medical sales rep who was home on maternity leave, and this motherhood thing wasn't going the way I had planned. (I can hear the moms out there laughing at that one!) First of all I had had no interest in breast-feeding. The convenience of bottle-feeding sounded much more up my alley. But my husband was a medical student at the time and was sold on the benefits of breast milk. The entire time I was pregnant, he would leave articles about breast-feeding tacked up all over our home.

So you see, I was pushed into breast-feeding by guilt. Little did I know I would take to it like a duck to water. I produced more milk than our growing daughter could possibly consume. Our freezer was bulging with all the little pouches of extra milk. There was no room for anything else. That's also what got my brain spinning. "We need some space."

I was healing from a C-section as well as some ligaments I tore while pulling my dogs away from chasing the neighbor's dog. I wasn't working for the first time in my life and I was bored. I definitely didn't want to spend the extra time cleaning my house, so I played around on my computer as I considered the breast milk idea.

I had no M.B.A., no nonprofit experience, and certainly not a sliver of an idea of how you would actually ship something as fragile as breast milk to Africa. So I did a Google search and came across two interesting items. One was a UNICEF chart that said that children orphaned by disease in Africa were six times more likely to survive if they were breast-fed. I thought, "I have to get my milk to these little orphans because they don't have a mom to provide for them."

> Our freezer was bulging with all the little pouches of extra milk. That's what got my brain spinning. We needed space!

I also found an article about a breast milk bank in Durban, South Africa. I emailed the bank and said I had milk to spare and wanted to send it.

A representative responded, asking if I had misread the article. The bank was in *Africa*! "Exactly," I said. "That's the whole point."

The representative said I should forget about it. It didn't make sense. It would cost too much money to ship properly. It had never been done before.

I said not to worry about it. I would do all the research on my end and see if it would even be possible. I called around to shipping companies and found out it would cost about $2,000. I was willing to pay that. It was worth $2,000 to me to see this milk not go down the drain. As it turns out, I didn't have to pay.

It just so happened that the milk bank coordinator's husband had some business in Chicago. So I packed up the extra milk on dry ice, drove to Chicago from my home in Columbia, Missouri, and met him. He was able to check my box filled with breast milk and dry ice as a piece of his luggage. It arrived in Africa the next day. That was essentially the first shipment.

Two days later I was seeing pictures of these little babies in Africa drinking my milk. It brought tears to my eyes. The world can seem such a big place, but it gets so small with the Internet and air travel.

That one shipment was about 1,000 ounces, which can provide

30 ounces of milk to one baby for 30 days. It was also the start of a project bigger than I could have imagined.

Our local newspaper ran an article, and suddenly I was overwhelmed with calls from other mothers who wanted to donate their milk to Africa too. I figured I'd better set up some kind of system fast.

Two weeks later I had a second shipment ready to go. This time it also included milk from two other moms, totalling 3,000 ounces. DHL donated the shipping. I thought, "Wow. That was great. That was my contribution to the world. I'm done."

As luck would have it, ABC News was in South Africa doing a story at the same orphan clinic at the same time the milk shipment arrived. The story went from focusing on the clinic to include the milk arriving from the United States. Once the ABC story ran, this movement became unstoppable. Within a few days I had more than 1,000 emails from people all over the world wanting to donate milk.

This was going to take a much bigger operation to handle. The problem was I had no experience in any of this. However, I've found that if you look around, you can find the help you need.

My brother was the first one to step up. He had already read several books on starting a nonprofit organization and had completed all the paperwork to start a nonprofit centered on organic farming. My brother helped me with the piles paperwork, which took several months, but now we are an official 501(c)(3) organization.

It's a good thing because about a month later we were mentioned on the *Oprah Winfrey Show*, and then things were out of control because of all the interest. It went from me as the single donor to processing more than 2,000 applicants in a little over a year. We went from sending 1,000 ounces to more than 50,000!

I learned it's one thing to have a great idea. It's another to let the idea grow and become a sustainable project. I needed to figure out a system that would protect both the moms and the babies and allow this project to continue for the long term.

I found a great corporate partner with the bioscience company Prolacta Bioscience. I found the company the same way I started this whole project—with a Google search. Since all donor moms must pass a blood test, Prolacta sends a phlebotomist to each of their homes so they never have to leave the house. We ship coolers to their homes, and Prolacta pasteurizes and tests the milk. We must have the highest safety standards or this won't work.

We've also found another wonderful partner in Quick International Courier, a company that specializes in critical shipping materials and impossible deadlines. Quick is providing all of our shipping to Africa for free.

> It's one thing to have a great idea. It's another to let the idea grow and sustain a project. I needed to figure out a system.

All this fast growth has brought another challenge that I had no experience with, blogger criticism. Some of it was just people wondering if such good things can happen in the world. Some of it, though, has been very helpful. It has helped me focus on what I'm trying to achieve here and what is best for the babies I'm trying to help in Africa.

I realize now that there is a better model than just shipping endless ounces of breast milk from the United States to Africa. Ship some milk but also send money to develop local health care. This way we will be maximizing our ability to reach more infants in need.

In our new business model, Prolacta processes 25 percent of the milk that comes in for Africa; 75 percent stays here in the United States. Prolacta will give the International Breast Milk Project $1 per ounce so that we can use that money to develop health care infrastructure.

Some people get cynical when they see a for-profit company and a nonprofit organization working together. But it's the only way for something like this to move forward.

When I look at the plans we have and all that's possible, it blows my mind that it all started with my staring at a lack of freezer storage space. We now empower mothers to become overnight philanthropists. Most moms don't have $5,000 to donate, but many do have 5,000 ounces of breast milk. Those donations empower them to make a difference. The International Breast Milk Project has now become my obsession. It sometimes drives my husband crazy, but I remind him that this all started with his putting those articles up around the house encouraging me to breast-feed in the first place.

If you have a good idea to improve the world but not a lot of know-how or even support, go for it! At the very beginning many people thought I was crazy, including my husband, my parents, and the milk bank in South Africa. When people doubt you, keep telling them and yourself, "Why not?" **For more go to breastmilkproject.org.**

Daryn's Takeaways

Jill is a perfect example of someone who doesn't let lack of know-how get in her way. She knew nothing about starting a nonprofit and had never been to Africa. Yet she listened to her passion and inspiration more than to her critics.

This is a good time to introduce my concept of the energy budget. The way I see it, I have two budgets. My financial budget, the limited resources I have in the bank, dictates how much I can spend on my business.

I also have a set amount of energy I can spend each day. I simply choose not to spend my energy on the critics. This is not to say that I don't listen to advice. Rather I simply consider listening to naysayers and negative people to be a very poor energy investment, the equivalent of throwing money out the window.

How are you spending your energy budget each day?

Saving the Children

Bob Nameng,
former street child and founder of
Soweto Kliptown Youth (SKY)

I was an orphan living on the streets of South Africa's slums. A wonderful woman gave me a second chance at life. Now I choose to live among and serve children who are in the same position I was. I've dedicated my life to giving them the second chance I was lucky enough to receive.

Kliptown probably means nothing to you, but it's the worst of the worst ghettos in South Africa. It's a squatter's camp of stick tents, torn-up cloth and dirty cardboard, and various old ramshackle and rusting tin shacks.

AIDS is more prevalent here than any other place in Africa. Crime is rampant. A young Kliptown girl's first sexual experience has a one in three chance of being rape. Raw sewage runs through the streets. Electricity is sporadic because people steal the copper electric cables for food money. Many die attempting to do this. Kliptown is a hell on earth.

But it's my home and my life. I've never been far from here. My parents were separated when I was 4, and my dad died when I was 6. I never saw my mother again, but I was told she died. I pray every day, even now, that God will bring her back to me. I had two brothers, one older and one younger, but they also died. I was basically left here in this squalor to fend for myself among the depressing shacks and heaps of garbage.

After I was orphaned I lived on the streets for 2½ years. I guess you could say that my life was nothing but obstacles, and I learned at an early age to be a survivor.

I was found by a saint of a woman whose name was Eva Mokoka. Eva took me in and showed me kindness and gave me a sense of security I'd never known before. Without her I'm sure I'd be dead because life in the streets is do or die. And most young people die. She taught me about God and faith and how to look forward to a future. In a place like this, such hope is almost unheard of. It changed me.

I went to grammar school and high school, but most of my education was on my own. I've always believed that intelligence is in you, and you just have to believe enough in yourself for it to come out.

I became deeply immersed in music, particularly the music of Bob Marley, whose songs I found to be infused with powerful and meaningful lyrics. Music has probably helped me in my work here in Kliptown as much as anything. It's a language that reaches lost kids. Music, art, writing, and poetry are therapeutic, and they are a large part of what I do to help these kids feel like they matter.

I was 16 when I first began helping young people. There were so many needs and few or no resources. Because of this I had to use my own. As I often say, God will never give us more than we can bear, which means that we all have what it takes in our minds and souls and hearts. For me the secret to getting at these resources was spending time alone, meditating, becoming aware of myself, building my confidence, and becoming my own best friend. I discovered that I was unique, powerful, different, and special in my own way, just like everybody is. That's when I started to understand the story of Jesus feeding thousands and thousands of people with just two loaves of bread and a few fish. If he could do that, why couldn't I?

I took that attitude and used it to create Soweto Kliptown Youth (SKY). Originally all the programs were run out of the back of an old tire-repair shop in my neighborhood of Meadowlands, but the organization grew. Today it is a collection of community programs, including AIDS awareness, child abuse and rape prevention programs, a shelter for the neglected, a charity collection, a youth theatre, soccer teams, and even beauty pageants. SKY even provides beds for children who need to spend a few nights away from abusive parents. The beds aren't much more than dirty old cushions on the floor, but they serve the purpose.

Despite overwhelming odds that face SKY even to this day, my staff and I just celebrated our 21st anniversary. Through all the poverty and filth, dirt, depression, shantytown shacks, hunger, abuse, and brokenness, we're somehow able to make it less grim for these forgotten kids.

> I was an orphaned street child, worthless in the eyes of the world, but I was given a second chance.

We've had so many successes. One example is Zoleka Cumbi. Zoleka grew up in SKY, and she is now a professional dancer. She went to the dance school Moving Into Dance in nearby New Town. That took her to Umoja, a powerful theater group that has toured the world, including London and Portugal, and soon will be traveling to Canada, the United States, and other places. Zoleka is a shining example of what anyone can accomplish if he or she has faith in himself or herself and works hard.

Several other SKY graduates have emigrated to America and send aid back to us. They call themselves Sisters of the Circle. We also receive kind and generous support from the Timberland Corporation, whose CEO, Jeff Swartz, has helped us with fundraising and with meeting the kids' material needs. And thanks to help from the National Basketball Association, which helps SKY financially, my staff and I are able to provide, on most days anyway, the very basics for our kids. We are deeply indebted to the kindness of the NBA, whose contributions keep us alive.

I've devoted myself to telling the world what's going on in Kliptown, Soweto, and other nearby ghetto areas of South Africa. I'm also devoted to extending kindness, hope, and love to the young people here. The payoff for this effort is a country that is fundamentally changed, recharged with hope for its people, with fairness and opportunities for everyone.

I was a neglected and orphaned street child, worthless in the eyes of the world, but thanks to a kindhearted woman I was given a second chance. I've made the most of it, and I won't let any child suffer what I had to suffer through. These kids are priceless. These kids are our kings and queens.

For more on Bob's work go to sky-foundation.org.

Desperate Escape

Paula Lucas,
founder and executive director of the
American Domestic Violence Crisis Line

If you're an American citizen living overseas and the victim
of domestic violence, you have all the power of the U.S. government
available to get you and your children back to safety. At least that's what I
thought. I was wrong. But I vowed if I could get out, I would help other
women and children fighting for their lives.

For a while I thought I was living a dream life. Soon after college
I met and married a dashing international photojournalist. We met in
San Francisco and soon moved to England and then to the United Arab
Emirates (UAE).

The move seemed to make sense since both my parents had died and
his family of Palestinian descent was living in Dubai. Looking back now, I
can see that the move was the beginning of a very dark time.

Even from the first day we arrived, my husband's charming demeanor
seemed to change. I can remember being in the living room with a bunch
of his relatives. They were all speaking in Arabic, which I didn't understand.
They were trying to talk to me and seemed to be talking about me. I went
to find my husband in another room and told him, "Your family is speaking
in Arabic. I can't understand a word they are saying."

He replied, "Well, if you don't like it, there's the door." Oh, if it were only so simple to leave. At that time I didn't feel like I had any family to come home to.

His anger and the abuse accelerated. When my first son was 6 months old, he picked him up and threw him against the crib. We would fight and argue. He would apologize and cry. I wanted to believe things were going to get better, thinking any relationship had good and bad times.

Within a few years I had three sons. My husband's whole focus during this time was getting an American passport for himself. As a Palestinian, he traveled on Lebanese travel documents. He believed his whole world would turn around when he had an American passport. I believed things would improve, that his anger and temper would subside.

Actually it turned out exactly the opposite. My husband's American passport came through at the end of 1995. That's when the real hell began. It was as if he was empowered. He didn't need me anymore, and the physical abuse escalated.

In 1997 I had a huge wake-up call. We were in a car accident that I believe my husband caused on purpose. Doctors said they wanted to keep me in the hospital overnight for observation. My husband refused. In Arab countries the woman can't say anything. Her husband has the final word. So he took me out of the hospital.

He also stepped up abuse of the kids. Dinnertime was the worst. If they wouldn't eat their food, he would shove it down their throats. Often he made them eat their own vomit.

That was it. I called the family that I did have left and for the first time shared that abuse was happening. I needed to get out and couldn't take it anymore. I went to the American Embassy for help. My family called the State Department. Everyone kept saying the same thing, "There's nothing we can do. If we help you, we'll create an international incident."

I learned there are offices at American embassies to help U.S. citizens if they are the victim of a crime like rape, kidnapping, or murder. But in many countries domestic violence is not illegal, so officials' hands are tied.

The nightmare went on like this until 1999, when I saw a chance to escape. My husband was traveling in Europe when he was robbed. All of his travel papers, money, and passport were stolen. He wouldn't be able to get back into the UAE without them. This was my chance.

My husband had hidden the boys' passports, thinking that would keep me from going anywhere. I turned the house upside down and finally found them. But I had no money. So I forged a check from a business account for $5,000 cash. I bought plane tickets for the four of us from Dubai to the United States.

I also needed travel documents giving me permission to leave the country with the children. If I was caught leaving without my husband's permission, I would be put in prison. Even though my husband was Christian, we were in an Islamic country under Islamic law. So I forged the documents that I needed.

> If I was caught without travel documents, I would be put in prison for leaving without my husband's permission.

There I was, after 15 years of marriage, fleeing with one suitcase and my kids, ages 4, 6, and 8.

The first six months my kids and I stayed in a variety of domestic violence shelters and at friends' homes, living on welfare and food stamps. We were trying to stay a step ahead of my husband, who was fighting for custody and trying to force us back to the UAE.

I was naive. I thought, "I'm American. My kids are American. I'm home. I'm done. I'm free." I hired a lawyer who said, "You can file for separation and custody of the kids, but he's fighting for jurisdiction."

"What the heck does that mean?" I wanted to know.

"It means he's trying to force you back to the Middle East, saying the country of UAE has jurisdiction over this case and Oregon does not."

It took a year and a half, but by late 2000 I was divorced and had full legal custody of my sons. I also had a $40,000 legal bill, all to protect my kids and keep them in their own country.

All along I had decided that I would help others still stuck in the same situation I had been in. I started the American Domestic Violence Crisis Line even before we moved out of the shelters. I wanted to give women someone to talk to, someone to offer them advice. For instance, during my custody battle my lawyer wanted to use photos of the boys when they had been abused. I had all that—back in Dubai. If only someone had told me that my case would have been so much easier if I had physical evidence. As it was, it was a case of "he said, she said."

To start, the crisis line was just a simple website, a place where women could send emails. In 2001 I added the International Domestic Crisis Line. It's toll-free from 175 countries and is confidential. We pay all the charges, and the call doesn't appear on the caller's phone bill.

Raising money has definitely been a challenge. I can't tell you how many of my grant proposals were turned down. Things brightened in 2002 when the crisis line won The Sunshine Peace Award, which acknowledges work in the domestic violence field.

On the plane to the ceremony, I sat next to a man who listened to my woes of grant rejections and fundraising. He said something so simple. "If what you're doing isn't working, then you need to do something else."

So I went back and researched women who were working on women's rights around the world. I wrote letters to five of them, asking for advice. Would you believe three of those women sent me money, including Yoko Ono, who sent me a check for $25,000?

Suddenly The American Domestic Violence Crisis Line was able to start 2003 with $60,000. We provided relocation funds for a family for the first time. We also provided a legal retainer for a family to file for custody.

I never thought this would go beyond a crisis hotline. I thought all I had to do was explain to women how to have all their ducks in a row: Bring photos, medical records, legal papers. But you can't just talk to people and then drop them if they don't even have the money for a plane ticket.

In 2006 alone, the American Domestic Violence Crisis Line took 1,286 crisis calls from 258 families in 47 countries. And we relocated 14 families back to the United States.

My dream is to keep helping more and more families. There are millions of Americans living overseas. If the domestic violence statistics in the United States are the same in other countries, that means as many as 40,000 women and 35,000 children are suffering abuse annually.

I understand better now how the embassies and the State Department have their hands tied with international diplomatic complications. So the American Domestic Violence Crisis Line now tries to work alongside American officials abroad to help women in ways the government can't.

When I came back to the United States, many people told me I needed to get a regular job and make money. Instead I took a job that paid very little so I could work swing shifts, be there for my children, and reach out to other women stuck where I had been. This is definitely where my heart wanted to go and where I will stay until I've helped as many women and families as I can.

The American Domestic Violence Crisis Line is a registered nonprofit organization. You can learn more at 866uswomen.org.

Bringing Babies to My House

Donna Carson,
social worker and founder, My House

I was a social worker in an overburdened, big-city hospital nursery who said, "Enough." Someone had to find a home for babies with nowhere to go. I looked around and saw no one doing anything. So with no money, no know-how, and only a fire in my belly, I decided to take these babies home to My House.

My House is a wonderful home in Atlanta for children who have been removed from their own families and who often have medical issues. It's a place that shows the power of unconditional love and the miracles that can happen when someone believes in a child on whom others have given up.

It was a long journey to reach this point. Most people sit around and wait for someone else to do something about a social problem. I decided I couldn't do that anymore.

My inspiration began as I toiled as a social worker in the neonatal intensive care unit at Atlanta's Grady Memorial Hospital. There were 100 beds of sick children and I, the only social worker. Over the years I noticed there were increasing numbers of children who didn't have anywhere to go when it came time for them to go home.

In the mid-1980s crack cocaine was coming on the scene. The hospital was getting very sick babies who had been delivered right inside crack houses. We had the medical technology to save these babies, but when it came time for them to leave the hospital, the mothers weren't involved or were still actively using drugs, and the babies had nowhere to go.

Those babies were in limbo. They were called boarder babies because although they were medically ready to leave the hospital, they had no home to go to, so they stayed at the hospital. They boarded. Foster parents could rarely take the babies in because they often had special medical needs. For a healthy baby, it can be hard to find a foster home. For these medically fragile babies, it is virtually impossible.

> We had the medical technology to save these babies, but when it came time for them to leave the hospital, they had nowhere to go.

By 1990, 45 percent of the babies admitted to the hospital nursery had cocaine in their systems. I was serving families who were very poor, weren't receiving prenatal care, and were delivering 1-pound babies. I felt like I was drowning. I didn't know anything about raising money or starting programs. But I've discovered that if you learn enough, if you have common sense and good intuition, and if you care enough, you can succeed.

My intuition told me I needed to find the mothers while they were still pregnant. I was able to secure a $500,000 grant to launch Project Prevent. My team and I hit the streets finding pregnant addicts, getting them into treatment, and getting them good health care so they didn't deliver sick babies. Within the first year Project Prevent reduced the drug incidence in the intensive care nursery to 11 percent!

In the 10 years that program operated, my team and I served over 10,000 families in Atlanta. We did a lot to reduce the number of boarder babies, but even with that, there was still more to be done. That's how I got the idea to start My House.

I wanted to create a place where these babies could one day say with pride, "I lived here." It took a year and a half to get approval from the state because I was proposing a nontraditional way of doing things. Basically I wanted to provide around-the-clock unconditional love for babies that nobody wanted. I would rely on a small staff and a team of volunteers to take care of the children and keep My House running.

I started with babies who were drug exposed because that's what I knew. But once My House opened, we began to take in all kinds of children, from those who needed liver transplants to kids who had been abused and siblings of kids who had medical problems.

I was so naive when I started. I thought the babies would only be at My House a few months. I didn't even buy a stove because I thought all we would need was milk and formula. We heated the milk and formula in a microwave oven and used a countertop unit to sterilize bottles.

My House now keeps the kids up until they are 5 years old. The grocery bill is $150 per week. And, yes, after four years we finally got the stove.

We take care of all their needs, both physical and emotional. We do everything you would do for a child in your own home, but we have 12 children at a time.

Most people who come into My House say it feels like their grandmother's house—it feels like home. You rarely hear any of the babies crying because they're usually in somebody's arms. Between the 350 volunteers and the staff, the children are constantly held and loved.

I worried about the children not having a primary mommy and daddy. That is so essential. But I've found that if you have 350 people always smiling at you, bringing you positive energy, and who are glad to be with you, miracles can happen.

My House has turned into a little laboratory that's testing the limits of doctors' dire predictions. For example, one little girl, appropriately named Hope, came to us at 3 weeks old. Her mother had done some unknown type of drugs while she was pregnant. When Hope came to My House, she was like a floppy, unresponsive doll. She wouldn't react to anything. She wouldn't look at toys or smile. Nothing. A top pediatrician assured us that she was blind and deaf. She was like that for months. Our staff and volunteers continued to shower her with love and attention.

Then around the time Hope reached 5½ months old, she started to blink. I know that sounds like a tiny thing, but to us it was a sign that somebody might be inside that body. Indeed there was. That was the beginning of some incredible events.

Today Hope is 5 years old. She is developmentally ahead of her age group in every realm. She also has a new family. One of our volunteers was a single woman with no intention of having kids. She was volunteering the night Hope came to My House and instantly fell in love with her, even when it looked like there was no hope for Hope. She did all the paperwork and required courses and became Hope's mother.

The creation of families is one miracle I didn't count on when I started all this. But just like Hope's new mother, we have volunteers falling in love, asking, "How can I become an option for this child?" About 80 percent of our kids go into adoptive homes when they leave here, often with our volunteers or staff.

In eight years My House has had 129 children. It's the best thing I've ever done. I get to witness the power of love every day. I was a very good social worker, but for me that felt like putting Band-Aids on some bad situations. Here I know I'm changing lives. These kids will have totally different lives because they came here. They will have a chance.

My House has not only saved lives but has also saved the county a lot of money. It costs about $1,500 a day to keep a child in a hospital, not including the cost of doctors and medicine. It costs My House about $200 a day to keep and love the same child.

> My House is the best thing I've ever done. I witness the power of love every day.

I'd love to replicate our program throughout the country or wherever there's a need for children to have a special place to go. As it is, we turn down anywhere from 5 to 15 kids a day. They simply need a good, safe place to be. There's something wrong with the fact that so many kids are in this situation.

To others who see problems that need to be fixed, I would encourage you to go for it. If it's not your job, then whose is it? Get to know a system and do enough research to know the specific need. Beyond that, you must have enough fire in your belly to say, "This is important to me! I'm going to do this!"

Don't wait for someone else to fix a problem. Roll up your sleeves, get to work, and spread the power of unconditional love. Miracles are right around the corner.

For more on My House go to myhouseweb.org.

Daryn's Takeaways

I love Donna because she saw important work that needed to be done and she didn't wait for the government or for someone else to fix the system. She simply looked around and figured, why not her?

She also didn't wait to have enough money or know-how. She rolled up her sleeves, got to work, and is amazed on a daily basis at how many people are willing to join her in her important work of caring for these special kids.

What social problem do you see that needs to be addressed? If you overlook lack of funds or expertise, what kind of impact could you make?

Sewing Up Inspiration

Garth Larsen,
cafe founder and father

When you don't like what's offered on the menu of
life, sometimes you need to cook up new things on your own. Everyone
knows life can sometimes serve up distasteful circumstances. When
the world didn't offer my physically challenged son employment
opportunities and a place to find purpose in life, I decided to create the
opportunity for him myself.

Back in the restaurant business is the last place I thought I would
ever be. But that's exactly where I am as I run Max's Positive Vibe Cafe
in Richmond, Virginia. My son, Max, inspired the creation of this place
so that he and others could have the kind of opportunity they weren't
receiving in the traditional workforce.

I first noticed something might be wrong with Max when he was
4 years old. His preschool teacher told us she didn't believe Max was
developing physically like other little boys. We had him checked out, and
doctors told us not to worry.

By the time Max was 8, we could no longer write off his inability to
run fast to not being an athletic kid. At this point his 3-year-old sister was
running laps around him.

We went for another round of testing. The final diagnosis was devastating. Max had a form of muscular dystrophy called Duchenne. It's one of the most common forms of the disease, and there is no cure or even a completely effective treatment. It's also a death sentence. All the research told us our sweet boy would die by his late teens or early twenties.

Indeed the disease did progress. As Max's muscles became weaker, he had to start using a wheelchair. All the friends he met through muscular dystrophy camp died, just as expected. But not Max.

He was now in his mid-twenties and still alive. That presented a different challenge. There's no guidebook on how you live life with a disability longer than anyone predicted. Max was so eager to be an active member of society, but he had an impossible time finding opportunities with his physical limitations. He would fill out applications for any number of things but never had any luck. Most people wouldn't even call him back.

This is when I became most concerned for my son. I had spent time volunteering with Meals on Wheels, and I had seen what can happen to disabled folks who give up hope on having a life. Their world seemed to narrow down to TV and a delivered meal. They had lost hope for anything more.

Max was never going to be a shut-in because we would take care of him. But he was definitely heading toward that feeling of giving up. I couldn't handle seeing that happen to my son. Rather than curse all those who wouldn't give my son an opportunity, I decided to investigate what I could create myself.

That's how I came up with the idea of opening a cafe. The irony was not lost on me. I was actually in the restaurant business many years ago, but I quit because it was taking too much time from being with my kids. Instead I started selling life insurance. Now here I was considering opening a restaurant business that would actually allow me to spend time with my son. Talk about coming full circle.

My son and I decided to call it Max's Positive Vibe Cafe. We would serve delicious lunches and dinners. Just as important, the cafe would raise money to help people with all kinds of disabilities—not just physical disabilities like Max's but also people with cognitive disabilities.

I actually thought this idea would be an easy sell to my community in Richmond. I was wrong. I thought it would take about a year to set up, but a year and a half later folks around here were just not catching on to this progressive idea. I had some board members who were mostly friends. We weren't having any success raising money or getting this idea across. Everybody gave up, even Max. But I didn't.

This is where all my years of selling life insurance came in handy. You hear "no" a lot in that line of work. After a time it stops bothering you. That's why I wouldn't let all the negative reactions about the cafe stop me. I simply didn't stop telling people about this great idea and asking for their support.

> I wouldn't let the negative reactions about the cafe stop me. I simply didn't stop telling people about this great idea.

My perseverance paid off. One and a half years into this project, I received the first sizable donation, $10,000 from the Target Corporation. People started to hear about us, and some articles appeared in the newspaper. People began to volunteer equipment and services.

The cafe was built in the same space where my insurance office used to be. We opened for business in January 2005. Looking back, I probably wouldn't have turned down a $300,000 grant check to get the cafe up and running. But this process has turned out to be so much better. You can't substitute the value of having so many people participate.

People from all walks of life contributed: attorneys, plumbers, electricians, construction workers, equipment people. They all feel they have ownership in this project and justifiably so. An electrician might come into the cafe for lunch, point up at a light fixture, and say, "I installed that." That kind of pride is something we wouldn't have if we had paid them to do the work.

We now have 25 paid employees. Seventeen of them have a physical or cognitive disability, but coming to Max's Positive Vibe Cafe isn't about watching people struggle. It's about wonderful service and delicious food. That's No. 1. This is a good restaurant.

Each of our employees has gone through our four-week training class. They learn how to bus a table and run a commercial dishwasher, how to present themselves at a job, and how to practice good sanitation and hygiene. It's as much about building confidence as it is about teaching skills.

We're simply trying to make it harder for employers to say no to these people. We have about a 40 percent employment rate outside the cafe. We do like to encourage graduates to seek work elsewhere so that we can make room for more trainees to come through. We're seeing acceptance throughout the Richmond community. Restaurateurs are saying, "If they've been through your program, we'll give them a shot."

One employee who isn't leaving is my son, Max. He comes in each day around 4 p.m. and runs the front of the restaurant. He seats people and is in charge of booking all the bands that play at the cafe. His weak muscles mean that he can no longer play an instrument, but he gets to live his love of music in this way.

He's 30 years old now, having lived twice as long as some doctors originally predicted. I honestly believe this cafe, giving him purpose in life, is the medicine that doctors said didn't exist for his condition.

Along the way, creating something for Max has also created opportunity for so many others as well. We've had more than 200 trainees go through our program. Watching them blossom from scared and bewildered to confident employees is the best payoff for me. I can see that the cafe has changed their lives. That new life is the most delicious thing we serve up!

I refused to let the world keep disappointing my son. I wasn't going to give him up to despair. If you feel life is selling you short, ask yourself, "What can I create to change this situation?" You'll have an incredible amount of hard work ahead of you, but just remember what those crazy people in Richmond cooked up. If we can do it here, why can't you?

To learn more about Max's Positive Vibe Cafe, visit positivevibecafe.com.

Daryn's Takeaways

· ·

For me, Garth and Max live the adage "create what you seek." So many people sit around bemoaning what's not in their lives—or at least longing for the day that it will arrive.

I admire people people like the Larsens, who stopped waiting for the world to create the opportunity they wanted for Max. Instead they created a place where Max could have the kind of job he wanted while at the same time helping out many other folks as well.

This idea of creating what you seek has gotten me out of many ruts. If you want love, then love. If you want inspiration, then go be inspiring. If you want abundance, be generous. It works every time.

What could you create that you might think is lacking in your life?

Creating Opportunity One Bite at a Time

Alicia Polak,
former investment banker and founder
of The Khaya Cookie Company

This is what they teach you in business school about baking cookies: not a crumb! Yet that's how I'm applying my M.B.A. skills today, running a cookie company that employs people from some of the poorest townships in South Africa. I walked away from a comfortable six-figure salary to go make the world a better place.

To be fair, there were parts of being a powerful investment banker in New York City that I really enjoyed. It's a go-go career in which you make deals worth millions of dollars practically every day.

The job took me all across Europe, India, and Russia, and we always traveled first class. There I was, Alicia Polak from Cinnaminson, New Jersey, jet-setting around the world and hobnobbing with zillionaires.

I also really enjoyed the salary. My family had little money when I was growing up, and I worked as a lifeguard and legal assistant all through school to help pay for college. Now for the first time in my life, I had money. Plenty of it. I could pay the bills when they came in—I could even overpay if I wanted to.

And yet something was missing. Call me idealistic, but growing up I always wanted to make a difference in the world. It didn't feel like that was happening as I sat behind my desk every day.

I was dragging myself to work, and I realized my heart just wasn't in it anymore. Logic told me to stay in the job and bank a bunch of money for my security. But there's always a difference between logic and my stomach. My stomach knew it was time to go.

In 2001 I was in Cape Town, South Africa, as an exchange student while working on my M.B.A. I saw people living in shacks amid the worst kind of poverty and knew this is where I wanted to make my mark.

I quit my job, packed my things, and headed to Africa.

I thought the answer was working with a nonprofit organization that was distributing battery-free radios. The radios are a wonderful tool for spreading information during crises such as floods or political instability.

Great idea, but not my final stop. For me the radios were about giving something away. It's like the old saying "Give a man a fish; he'll eat for a day. Teach a man to fish; he'll eat for a lifetime." I wanted to create "fishing poles," a way to pass along empowering job skills to the poorest South Africans.

> For the first time the women could make the connection between their hard work and what was on the store shelves.

One day the inspiration came to me. "Cookies! I'll start a cookie company!" I thought. "I'll create opportunity one bite at a time!" Keep in mind, I knew as much about baking cookies as you learn on the back of a chocolate chip bag.

Here is where my background as an investment banker came in handy. I had had excellent schooling and good training from some great bosses. If you can run an initial public offering, you know how to execute very quickly. I located the people I needed to meet, including a pastry chef and a food scientist to help me formulate the recipes. You don't need to know how to make cookies if you can find and hire people who do.

The intention was to set up shop in Khayelitsha, one of the poorest townships just outside Cape Town, and hire women who otherwise wouldn't have jobs.

The challenges to my "Save the World" mentality began almost right away. The cultural differences were immense, none bigger than the concept of time. I was coming from the investment banking world where everyone expected everything 20 minutes ago. My first hires weren't even interested in showing up to work on time, if at all.

Then there was the issue of the burned cookies. Every day there would be batches and batches of burned cookies. I couldn't understand it. I had clearly written the number of minutes the cookies were supposed to bake. I figured, a number is a number. It shouldn't matter whether you speak English, Afrikaans, or Xhosa, their home language.

Finally it hit me: People think about time differently in Africa. These women did not live with clocks in their homes or even wear watches. I bought everyone on the staff a watch, and we moved on from there.

I also had to overcome the women's distrust of me. I think they figured I was just another white do-gooder and nothing would come of this venture. But I slowly won them over by working as hard as they did. I didn't ask the women to do anything I wasn't willing to do myself. When the floors needed to be mopped, I mopped. I lugged large sacks of flour. At first suppliers wouldn't come into the township to deliver our raw materials because the area was considered too dangerous. So I would forage and gather our goods.

Still I didn't feel like they were completely understanding the whole concept. So one day I said, "That's it. Everyone in the *bakkie!*" That's the Afrikaans word for "truck." I drove the women about 40 miles outside the township. For some of them, it was the first time in their lives they had been that far away from home.

We drove to the local supermarket where Khayelitsha cookies were sold. For the first time the women could make the connection between their hard work and what was on the store shelves.

I could see their sense of pride swelling right there in the supermarket aisle. That's the day things began to turn around. They understood why quality was so important; they saw for themselves why the labels had to be straight. Most important, they could see their own power to create.

Today you can find Khayelitsha cookies in hotel boutiques and stores across South Africa. I sold the Khayelitsha Cookie Company to locals and launched the Khaya Cookie Company to sell our brownies, granola bars, and shortbread treats all across America. Because of special packaging we are able to make them in South Africa and ship them to the United States without using any preservatives. Every time a customer takes a bite of a Khaya cookie, he or she is creating opportunity for men and women thousands of miles away.

The sweetest thing of all has been to see the transformation in these women's lives. Women who barely showed up to work when I started are now essentially running the bakery. Each woman is responsible for her own type of cookie, and they feel a sense of ownership over those recipes.

This has all been a nice start to my original goal. I know I can't save the entire world, but I can tell you without a doubt there is a group of women in South Africa whose lives have a higher quality because of the skills and confidence they've learned. For me that's what makes it all worthwhile. Otherwise, having a cookie company is actually much harder work than investment banking.

There are things I miss about banking—it would be fun to splurge now and then on a pair of fancy shoes and not even care about the price. Splitting my time between South Africa and Philadelphia can be exhausting as well. But there's no going back. I've definitely found my purpose. The same stomach that told me it was time to leave banking now delights in sampling what I think are the world's best treats.

My big dream is to re-create this business model in low-income communities here in the United States. Again the goal is to empower people with job skills instead of making them depend on handouts.

For any of you who have that dream of walking away from your high-powered, high-paying job but think you can't: Remember, there is no such word as "can't." Take it from me, you can choose to walk away and go for your dream. The payoff will be so much sweeter than the fattest paycheck.

Find out more about Alicia Polak and Khaya cookies at khayacookies.com.

The Castaway Daughter

Marilyn Tam,
former child laborer and current world humanitarian

You don't hear many stories of child laborers

who grow up to change the system. Yet that is exactly my journey and my story. I've found that life is all about using what you have to make your dreams come true, no matter who you are or where you begin your life.

I was born in Hong Kong to a traditional Chinese family, the second daughter followed by three sons. That meant my worth to my family wasn't very high. They thought nothing of sending me to live out in the country with my aunt and uncle, who didn't have any children of their own.

I wish I could tell you that going to my aunt and uncle's house meant being embraced by a couple who longed to love a child. They had good intentions, but they had busy lives as they both worked. I spent most of my time with their maid and her adopted daughter.

At my aunt and uncle's house, I learned to assemble bunches of plastic flowers; assembling 100 stems earned $1. My small hands were also considered good for doing needlepoint for fancy needlepoint handbags. I earned 75¢ for each piece.

No one called it child labor or felt sorry for you. It was just what you did.

When I was 11 years old, my aunt finally got pregnant, and I was sent back to Kowloon, Hong Kong, to live with my family. They still were not very interested in me, and I spent most of my time reading and being outdoors in nature. I was fascinated with *National Geographic* magazine and I envisioned helping the people pictured there have better lives.

I attended a Catholic school, where I had a life-transforming experience. I wanted a classmate's address in order to send her a Christmas card. She wouldn't give it to me, no matter how much I badgered her. She finally told me that she was ashamed of where she lived. Five members of her family lived in one room and had to share a bathroom and kitchen with two other families.

I couldn't believe it. It didn't seem right that two working parents could only produce enough income for that kind of living situation. Reflecting on my early childhood experience and my friend's living conditions, I made a vow. I decided I would make a difference in the world. That was my life mission, and it's a promise I've kept to this day.

> No one called it child labor. It was just what you did.

Halfway through 10th grade, I came to America. One of my sisters was studying here, and I was ready to get started on my life mission. I went to the University of Oregon and Oregon State, finishing my undergraduate and graduate degrees in four and a half years.

My goal was to join the World Health Organization so I could go to Africa and help people learn about good nutrition and proper governance. When I was told I needed at least 10 years of experience prior to joining, I was crushed and I realized I needed to get another job.

I went down to the university career center and found out about a company called the May Department Stores. I had never heard of them, even though they were one of the major department store companies in the United States. I figured this would be a good place to practice interviewing because if I messed up, it wouldn't matter.

I learned that this company promoted workers based on merit. What a concept! I was a young immigrant, a small woman, and Asian. I had been discriminated against based on all of those factors at one time or another. This could just be the company for me!

The stores were using a new technology called point-of-sale computers to measure sales and productivity. You received immediate feedback every day on how you performed. I would be rewarded on what I accomplished rather than what I looked like.

Plus this company was generous with community service and open to discussion with its warehouse staff on unionization. Working for this company offered me a different way of looking at my new life. I might not be able to help the people in Africa, but I could make a difference right now with the people around me.

I thrived with May. I quickly went from executive trainee to corporate buyer in less than three years. My career in retail and manufacturing took off from there.

I was hired away by company after company. I worked with Britannia Jeans. Remember those patchwork jeans so popular in the late '70s? I was the director of design and development.

One day I received a call from Phil Knight, the founder of Nike. He wanted to open Nike concept retail stores. He had heard that I had a strong background in managing retail stores and wanted to talk to me about it.

I did my research. I could see that Nike shoes performed well, but the company's apparel and accessories were of uneven and often poor quality. The colors didn't match. The shrinkage factor wasn't good. The sizing wasn't consistent.

So faced with the opportunity to get this dream job and uncertain about the feasibility of the concept, I simply told Phil Knight the truth. I told him I couldn't take the job knowing the variability and unreliability of the merchandise. I explained my position and said, "I would love to work with you, but I don't think you can open a store right now." The interview ended shortly after that. I thought I had really blown it.

Three weeks later my phone rang. It was Phil Knight. "I've been thinking about what you said," he said. "You're right. Please come join the company as the vice president of apparel and accessories. Fix the merchandise, and then we'll open the stores."

After working with Nike for a while, I left to start my own consulting company back in California. A few years later I joined Reebok as the president of its apparel and retail group. Here I was really able to make an impact, changing the work conditions, age limits, and pay scales for apparel factory workers in developing countries. No company wants someone telling it how to run its business. But the buying power of a big company like Reebok gave me leverage. And I never forgot where I had come from. I knew what it was to work in those conditions because of my experience as a child laborer. No other executive knew what it meant to work like that.

The bottom line is I was able to show the factory owners that good working environments make for good business. Give workers better lighting, ventilation, and breaks, and hire workers of the proper age, and you will get better quality goods and on-time delivery!

We worked with our competitors and together we started making positive changes. It caused a great transformation in the apparel industry.

That's how my childhood experience came full circle.

Now I've moved on from Reebok. I usually stay at a job as long as it takes to make a positive difference in that arena. I've remained very clear about my mission in life.

> I was able to show factory owners that good working environments make for good business.

I've been able to do more work by forming my own nonprofit organization, The Us Foundation. We are working to create more harmony and understanding between people and people and between people and the planet. We work in many areas of the world. For example, in India we provide health care and education to children; in the southern United States we are helping in the area hit by Hurricane Katrina; in Sri Lanka we're helping communities damaged by the tsunami.

It's a very small foundation. I do, however, have a big Rolodex. My effectiveness lies in being able to make connections and create synergies between groups and individuals to get things done and make a difference.

I also speak and consult with Fortune 100 companies on leadership, diversity, change management, and integrating social and environmental concerns into a business profitably. It is a privilege to support other companies in their efforts to make a positive difference in the world.

I've learned a lot over my life's journey. I've learned it's possible for a neglected little Chinese girl to rise to power in some of the biggest companies in the world.

I've learned it's vital to always tell the truth, whether that means telling the truth to a powerful businessperson or staying true to your vision for your life.

And I've learned that even when life doesn't take you in the exact direction you expected, there's still room to make a difference and improve the world. It's all about using what you have to make your vision come true.

You can learn more about Marilyn Tam and her new book, *How to Use What You've Got to Get What You Want,* **at howtousewhatyouvegot.com. Learn more about The Us Foundation at www.UsFoundation.org.**

Proved Innocent

Ken Wyniemko,
wrongfully convicted former inmate and justice crusader

I spent almost 10 years in prison on rape charges. Like many prisoners I claimed my innocence, but in my case it was eventually proved true. This is the story of how I made it through that legal nightmare and why today I dedicate my life to helping free other wrongfully charged men and women.

My life took a radically bad turn on a nice summer day in July 1994. I was in bed at home in a suburb of Detroit called Clinton Township. I heard a knock on my front door and got out of bed. I opened the door to see a young lady in a business suit standing there. I asked if I could help her, and she asked me if my name was Kenny. I said yes.

At that she stepped aside and two police officers came out of nowhere and tackled me. They threw me down on the floor of my living room and handcuffed me behind my back. They told me that I was going to be taken down to the station and placed in a police lineup.

There had been a rape 10 weeks earlier, and they thought I did it. I complained that they had made a terrible mistake, but they dragged me off to a squad car idling in my driveway.

That day marked the end of my freedom for 9½ years.

At the time this happened I didn't know much about the law. I did know that I was entitled to talk to an attorney. The lead detective apologized and told me that the attorney had left the building, but he said, "It's all right. You'll be released when this is all over."

First I had to stand in a lineup, and we were all asked to say, "What time does your husband come home?" That is what the rapist allegedly said to the victim.

Four or five hours later I was released, but that didn't last long.

When I arrived home a police cruiser was sitting in my driveway. The lead detective got out of the car and approached me and asked, "What are you doing?"

"Going inside to take a shower," I told him. My skin was crawling from the whole experience, and I couldn't wait to scrub it off.

He informed me that I couldn't do that because they were waiting for a search warrant to go through my house. I was so mad about this whole mess that I told him that it was my house, I was going inside to take a shower, and he was welcome to come in.

As I put my key in the door lock, he pulled his service pistol and pointed it at my head. I had never had a gun pointed at me, and I froze.

This all unfolded in front of my 76-year-old father, who had picked me up from the police station and taken me home. He had severe diabetes and started shaking uncontrollably and crying as he witnessed all this. He quickly suggested I just come to his house to take a shower, which I did.

When I returned to my home, it looked like a tornado had hit. All my things were ransacked and broken. I had no choice but to leave the place looking like that because I had to go to my job running a bowling alley. That was my last day at work.

I came home to find two lead detectives and four police cars waiting for me. They told me to drop my bags and spread-eagle against the car. Within seconds I had 10 guns pointed at me. They told me I was identified in the lineup and that I was under arrest.

I tried to tell them they had the wrong man. But they just treated me like dirt. The lead detective kept calling me the "million-dollar man."

"What does that mean?" I asked.

"By the time I get through [expletive] with you," he explained, "it's going to cost you a million dollars to get your [expletive] out of prison.

He was wrong. It took much more than a million dollars to reverse this tragic mistake. That was 1994. I didn't see freedom again until 2003. It took that long to prove my innocence.

I'm going to compress a very long and sad story. I was placed in the county jail, arraigned, charged. A trial was set for October. I didn't have money to hire a good attorney, so I was assigned a court-appointed attorney. I saw that man a grand total of two times.

My lawyer later resigned from the case, and the judge appointed a new attorney, who somehow managed to be worse than the first. When I complained, the judge told me that if I didn't like his choice I could defend myself.

> I kept insisting I was innocent, but nobody believes you when you're charged, even though the evidence against me was nonexistent.

I kept telling these people I was innocent, but nobody believes you when you're charged, even though the evidence against me was nonexistent.

For example, the rape victim identified me from a lineup, but the police report said her assailant, who was masked, woke her from a sound sleep and put a blindfold on her. She never got a good look at the guy. The report also said the only thing she could see was that the assailant had a cleft chin, was about 6 feet 2 inches, 220 pounds, and probably about 30 years old. I don't have a cleft chin, I was 5 feet 10 inches, 185 pounds, and 43 years old.

Semen found at the scene belonged to someone with type O blood. I have type A. There were no fingerprints.

But prosecutors had a jailhouse snitch testify against me. He said I admitted I raped that woman. It turns out they offered the guy a deal. If he would testify that I confessed, he would have all his charges dropped.

That testimony did me in. I was convicted on 15 counts of rape, 1 count of breaking and entering, and 1 count of armed robbery. The judge was put off that I showed no remorse, and he sentenced me to 40 to 60 years in prison, more time than many murderers get.

I was sent to Jackson State Prison in Jackson, Michigan. I spent every hour I could in the law library trying to find a way to win my freedom. The problem is that behind bars everyone claims to be innocent and to have gotten a raw deal, so nobody will listen to your pleas.

I sometimes wonder how I came out of the situation with any sanity at all. The truth is my faith pulled me through. I prayed constantly, and I believe God was there. I discovered that if you let your bitterness and anger run wild in you, it will destroy you. I'm thankful that, for whatever reason, I went in another direction and was able to keep focused and keep functioning.

I put together a compelling list of reasons why my case should be reconsidered and sent that list to every paper and media outlet in southeastern Michigan. It seemed hopeless. Then a friend suggested I contact Barry Scheck at the Innocence Project to get his help. The Innocence Project is a Cardoza Law School initiative to free wrongly imprisoned people. At that time Barry was in the middle of the O.J. Simpson trial and had received a bit of notoriety. After several months he kindly wrote back and said he had a 4,000-case backlog!

I was devastated, but I kept going. It took five years—five years—but finally my miracle occurred when a reporter named Kim North Shine at the *Detroit Free Press* read my pleas and decided to investigate.

It wasn't easy for her either. The Clinton Township police did everything they could to keep her from looking at the evidence. But more angels joined my case, including Michigan State law professor Kim Swedlow, the Innocence Project, and attorney Gail Pamokov.

Thanks to all of them, Kim Swedlow and Gail were finally granted access to the records. They uncovered one atrocity after another perpetrated by the police and the prosecutor's office. That included evidence that the lead detective withheld DNA evidence that would have cleared me. Despite the discovery the courts were still reluctant to overturn or retry my case.

Finally in 2001 Michigan law permitted DNA testing on old cases. I remember crying the night that became law. It still took some time, but on June 12, 2002, my DNA results came back.

On June 17, 2002, I finally walked out of prison.

Many people now ask me how cases like mine can happen. There are several reasons, including eyewitness misidentification, unreliable or limited science, false confessions, forensic science fraud or misconduct, government misconduct, informants or snitches, and just plain bad lawyering.

The Innocence Project estimates a 5 percent failure rate in the judicial system. I suspect that might be a low estimate. Still those numbers mean that 100,000 people are sitting in jails right now, wrongly convicted.

That's why my life goal is to help free these men and women and educate the public about what's going on. I'm often asked, "Why don't you just go lie on a beach somewhere and try to recover something of what was taken from you over those 10 years?"

The answer for me is simple: This is my recovery. I've always loved this country, and I've always been an honest person. I would never be able to look myself in the mirror, knowing that there's another innocent person just like me rotting in prison.

I did sue Clinton Township for wrongful imprisonment and settled out of court for a generous amount of money. That money gives me the freedom to do what I am meant to do: devote myself full-time to advocacy, speaking, and organizing for the Innocence Project at Michigan State's Cooley Law School.

One project began while I was still in prison and first learned about the DNA statute. The statute took effect on January 1, 2001, and was set to expire on January 1, 2006. When I became aware of the sunset date, I told myself, "Kenny, if you get out there is no way you can ever let that statute sunset."

I'm happy to say that on April 28, 2005, Governor Jennifer Granholm signed the extension. I was in her office when she signed the bill. She named the statute the Ken Wyniemko Law.

Part 5

Working Through Grief: Healing Acts

Art with a Heart

Lori Guadagno,
artist and surviving sister of United Flight 93 passenger
Richard Guadagno

Every day I provide art expression for chronically
and terminally ill children. It's my job at Wolfson Children's Hospital
in Jacksonville, Florida. And every day I thank those kids for saving my
life and helping me heal after the loss of my brother, Richard, who was a
passenger on United Flight 93 on 9/11.

I created the Art With A Heart For Children program with my cousin,
Lisa Ussery, back in 2001. We provide daily art experiences for kids who
are in the hospital fighting serious diseases such as cancer, cystic fibrosis,
and kidney failure. It often is the only joyful part of these children's day
and the only activity they can control.

The program grew out of a lifelong dream my cousin and I shared.
We grew up like sisters and we always wanted to do something significant
that would impact the world. I'm the artist; Lisa is great at all the
administrative duties and big-picture ideas.

Frankly we had no business creating this program. Neither one of us
is trained as an art therapist or art educator, nor do we have a background
in hospital work. But I've been an artist all my life, doing everything from
painting murals to decorating cakes. I've just always believed passionately

that art can save the day.

In early 2001 Lisa and I decided now was the time to create this special program and finally work together. There was only one problem: I was living in Vermont and Lisa lived in Jacksonville. Through a couple of connections, we were able to present our idea to the administrators at Wolfson Children's Hospital. We showed them how art could supplement medicine when it came to healing a sick child. It also helped that we had initial funding from the Fanny Landwirth Foundation lined up. Wolfson opened its doors to us.

We were set to launch in late fall 2001. There was just one important event before I packed and moved to Florida. Our beloved grandmother, Minnie, was turning 100! The entire family gathered in our New Jersey hometown for the celebration. That included Lisa, her family, my parents, and my only brother, Richard.

Truth be told, Richard was always Nana Minnie's favorite. He was the youngest of all the grandkids, and since Nana lived with us while we were growing up, Richard was always by her side. He was the sponge for her lifetime of stories and information about gardening, animals, and the great outdoors. It's not the biggest surprise that he grew up to be a biologist and wildlife manager for the U.S. Fish and Wildlife Service.

Richard was assigned to the Humboldt Bay National Wildlife Refuge in northern California. His job included all sorts of training I would never have imagined. He had to know firearms and hand-to-hand combat because there was no telling what kinds of characters he would come in contact with out in the wilderness. None of us could have imagined how that would lead to his final role.

Since he was coming so far across the country for Nana's party, Richard made a bigger trip of it, first spending a week with me in Vermont. Since my time there was coming to an end, he wanted to meet my friends and experience the rural countryside that had been my home. I am so thankful that my only sibling and I shared that magical week hiking, traveling around, and just hanging out together.

We drove down to Nana's birthday celebration. That was as wonderful as you can imagine, saluting an Italian-American grandmother whose greatest joy was to be surrounded by family.

Richard actually thought he was set to fly out Wednesday, September

12. He just happened to check his ticket only to discover he was booked for Tuesday, September 11. I'll never forget him saying, "Phew. I sure am glad that I checked the ticket! I would have missed my flight!"

I remember being so sad when I said goodbye to my brother. Since I would be living in Florida and he would be in a remote part of California, it would be a long time before I would see him again. I had no idea it would actually be the last time ever.

When the news started to break on that Tuesday morning, I was back at my job as a teaching assistant at a Vermont high school. Even as the teachers gathered around a television to watch the events unfold, it didn't occur to me that Richard could be on one of the affected flights. I pictured him sitting on the plane stuck on the tarmac at Newark, trying to figure out what was going on.

> We will never know for sure who did what on that plane, but my family has always been sure that Richard was one of the heroes.

But as the morning went on and I heard reports that one of the hijacked planes was an early morning plane from Newark to San Francisco, my panic level rose. Indeed, it was soon confirmed that my brother was on United Flight 93. That was the flight where it's believed a group of passengers overpowered the hijackers, forcing the plane to crash in a field in Shanksville, Pennsylvania, rather than let it destroy one of the intended targets in Washington, D.C.

We will never know for sure exactly who did what on board that plane. However, from the moment we heard the news my family has always been sure that Richard was one of the heroes who acted onboard. We know he had the proper training for his job and we know the kind of man he was. Miraculously Richard's wildlife service badge and his credentials somehow survived the crash. They were found near the cockpit.

I might be an artist, but there is no way to paint a picture of the grief and pain my family felt beginning that day. I lost my only sibling. It was even worse to watch my parents as they lost their only son. Up to this point in my life, I had never even experienced the death of any family member or close friend. Here I was grieving as part of a national tragedy.

This suddenly seemed the worst possible time to pick up and move to a new state and start a new life. I really thought I couldn't do it. And I almost didn't. Somehow I decided I could not *not* do it, and I'm so glad I did. Working with these special children has saved my life.

Each Art With A Heart session begins when I or another staff member enters the patient's room. From that point on, the child is in charge and calls the shots.

Patients can draw or paint, or if they are too sick to participate, they can tell me what they would like to see me create. Some describe a dream, a fantasy, or simply a pet. They enjoy just watching somebody do it, and it thrills them to see their vision become a reality. These children have no choice about their disease or treatment, but Art With A Heart sessions give them total control.

If these children want an actual learning experience, such as a formal art lesson, we can create that too. Ironically these kids are getting a better fine arts experience in the hospital than they are exposed to in school.

We watch the returning patients, those we call "frequent flyers," build a body of work. They go from being afraid to put a mark on a piece of white paper to painting on stretched canvas.

I look back at the creation of this program and realize just how naive my cousin and I were. We had no idea how intense it would be to work with seriously ill children. We thought it would be "We're here to do art! Yippee!"

In a surprising way my brother's death prepared me for this important work. These children look death in the face every day. Now, so do I. Before, I had no capacity to deal with death. I had great fear. Now, I'm working with kids who deal with it every moment of their lives. Together, we understand what it is to live on that edge.

I also have great compassion for the children's families. I understand their pain as seriously as the patient's. When I look in a sibling's eyes, I know what he or she is feeling and fearing about losing his or her brother or sister. It's one of the most horrifying losses. The kids, the parents, the siblings are experiencing much of the same pain that I have experienced.

Sometimes when it's appropriate I share my brother's story as an inspirational message about a hero. I don't use that term lightly because I know the word has been overused. But these children understand when

I use "hero" in reference to a real live human being in a story they are familiar with.

One young man was having a bone marrow transplant. Every day I would go to his room, which had to be a sterile environment. I would bring an item of my brother's, which would have to go through a complete alcohol wash. One day I brought him a bracelet from Shanksville. He wore that bracelet until the day he died because it gave him courage and comfort.

It's wonderful to be able to share the gifts of my brother's legacy with the children. The truth is I receive so much more from them than I could ever give. Working with these brave children every day forces me to be present in the moment. I don't think of anything else when I'm with them. I feel Richard's presence, and it's always positive, never sad. Sometimes as I leave work I wonder, "How can I call this a job when it's these kids showing me the way?"

> Working with these brave children every day forces me to be present in the moment.

It continues to amaze me that my cousin and I had established this program even before I knew how much I was going to need it. We listened to our instincts that this was good and important. So what if we didn't have a bunch of fancy degree letters after our names?

If you have an idea to improve the world around you but someone or something is trying to tell you that you aren't qualified, just trust your instincts. Ours told us Art With A Heart For Children was a good thing that was going to make a difference. We were right.

And for those of you drowning in the grief of losing a loved one, I know so well the pull to give in to the darkness. I certainly felt that overwhelming feeling after 9/11. Don't make that choice. It is so easy to sink into the misery of the moment. Even when it feels as if there is no other way to go, there is a choice. There is always a choice, and hopefully that choice is to move forward toward the positive. That's the choice I made when I turned to art and helping the children. That choice saved my life.

For more on Lori's work go to artwithaheart.info.

Daryn's Takeaways

. . . .

One word in Lori's story blows me away: choice.

Now she certainly didn't choose to have her brother die on Flight 93. What could make a sister feel more powerless than that? But Lori somehow realized that her power lay in how she dealt with her grief.

I've long believed that every challenging time, every heartbreak is an invitation to grow. You can choose to accept the invitation or not. I've had times when I accepted. And I've had times when I turned down the invitation.

I've also learned that you never really get to turn down the invitation completely, because if you don't accept this time, another opportunity is probably waiting just around the corner.

The awesome thing about Lori is that she not only chose to grow in her grief, she uses that to serve special children. Talk about an inspiration!

What are examples in your own life where you have grown from hard times? Have there been times when you chose to go toward the darkness of despair or grief, as Lori says? What happened to pull you back or point you in a more positive direction?

Ben's Bells

Jeannette Maré-Packard,
founder of Ben's Bells

I live with the pain of having watched my precious 3-year-old son die right in front of me. I've been inspired to channel that pain into a program that honors my son by promoting acts of kindness. Let me tell you about Ben's Bells.

I was living such a wonderful life in March 2002. I was a linguistics instructor at the University of Arizona, teaching sign language students to become interpreters.

More important, I was Mom to two wonderful little boys, Matt, 6, and Ben, 3. Ben was an outrageously bright, cheerful, energetic little boy. He was a precocious talker, loved music, and loved dancing naked. He loved to read, swim, and generally run around. He was an incredible light.

Whenever I tell the story of Ben's death, I always remark on what a regular day it was in my life. Ben had a cold. My husband and I weren't worried about him at all; all kids get colds, right?

We were home, and Matt had a friend over to play. Ben was happily playing along. He didn't have a fever or anything that we thought was too serious.

Then the next thing I knew, Ben was choking. His airway was closing off. He was standing right in front of me when it happened and he started turning blue. Immediately I was on the phone to 911 and trying to do CPR, but his airway was so acutely swollen that I couldn't get any air through.

The paramedics arrived and revived him, but our sweet Ben had been out too long. He died the next day in the hospital.

It turns out he had a croup virus, which is very common. Most of the time the croup is a fairly benign virus, but every once in a while, in situations like ours, it settles in and closes off the airway. That's what happened to Ben.

In an instant my life fell apart in ways I could never have fathomed. I was feeling pain that I could never have imagined was possible. For any parent the worst thing that can happen to you is to lose one of your children. Our trauma was only made worse in that we tried so hard to save him and failed. I found myself not knowing how to keep going. I guess every parent who loses a child feels that way.

Five months after Ben died I went back to work. Suddenly I was walking around the University of Arizona campus with 50,000 people swarming everywhere. It amazed me that I could be in so much pain and a person could walk right by me and not be able to tell. I always understood in my head that emotional pain is invisible, but once you're in it so deep and living it, it's amazing to see how the world continues on around you and how easy it is to hide your hurt.

I began to realize that if I was carrying around this pain and hiding it, then other people must be too. I began to look at people differently. For example, I would look at an 18-year-old kid and wonder if he was OK instead of just assuming he was.

At the same time, I was touched whenever anybody would do something kind for me. I mean any kind act: the simplest thing like opening up a door, or smiling at me, or saying "Good morning." Those seemingly small acts took on an entirely new significance. They became lifesaving for me.

When I felt that I couldn't keep going, someone would inexplicably do something kind, and I knew that I could keep going, at least for awhile.

That is how I knew that in Ben's memory I wanted to establish a project of kindness. I wanted people to realize that when they get up every day, they have dozens and dozens of opportunities to change the world in ways they don't realize. Anytime they do a kind act for a stranger, they set waves in motion. Those waves can heal people in deep places they secretly hurt.

My family and I created Ben's Bells as a way to set off those waves. Ben's Bells are beautiful ceramic wind chimes. We developed a design and started making them in our backyard studio with friends. The therapeutic effect of working with clay was amazing, as was the power of being surrounded by people talking and working toward a common goal. To each one we added a tag with our website and a message: "You've found a Ben's Bell. Take it home and remember to spread kindness."

> When you get up every day, you have dozens and dozens of opportunities to change the world in ways you don't realize.

March 29, 2003, was the first anniversary of Ben's death. On that day a group of volunteers helped us hang hundreds of our homemade Ben's Bells all over Tucson. We hung them in unexpected places where people would stumble across them and read the attached card.

That initial distribution was really for my family and me, but the response we received was unbelievable. It told us that we had to keep going.

We've now formed a nonprofit organization and distribute thousands of bells each year. Most recently we hung 500 here in Tucson and 500 in New Orleans. The impact of kindness is spreading in the strangest, most exciting places.

Ben's Bells have an extra magical quality in that you can't buy one. You either have to find one yourself or be nominated to receive a bell. We're very intentional about this. And the nomination piece of this project has been a huge hit! Each week we receive dozens of nominations and we have a committee that chooses one. Then we surprise that person at work, home, or wherever we can find him or her. We "bell" the recipient with a Ben's Bell, a T-shirt, and some other Ben's Bells "Be Kind" items. The recipients are featured in the local Tucson newspaper on Saturday.

As our program has grown, we have belled all kinds of regular people who are making the world better. We've belled school custodians, crossing guards, teachers, doctors, and lawyers.

The whole project has become a giant lovefest! I'm starting to reduce my workload at the university, and taking Ben's Bells nationwide will be my full-time job fairly soon. Many other cities are interested in Ben's Bells, and the organization's board of directors is working to figure out how to spread this simple message.

This project was born out of so much pain, but it has led me to meet tremendous people every day. That includes many people who are in a lot of pain themselves. We inspire each other and are motivated to do better even in the face of suffering.

The best part for my family? The bells are helping us heal, and they've been an incredible way for us to celebrate Ben each and every day.

Daryn's Takeaways

The key to Jeanette's story is how she and her family found healing by looking outside themselves.

It doesn't mean they didn't grieve or feel pain. But their own suffering was eased by bringing joy to and celebrating kindness in others.

There is a time to "feel the feel." And then there is a time to focus on others for our own benefit as much as theirs.

What act of kindness could you celebrate today?

Writer of Merit

Jacquelyn Mitchard,
best-selling novelist

I have felt grief so deep that I wanted to be the one who died instead of my husband. How could I know that his dying wish would lead me to become a best-selling novelist and the first selection ever for Oprah Winfrey's book club?

I was very pleased with the life I was living in 1993. My husband, Dan, and I were living in small-town Wisconsin. He was a reporter for the local paper. I had just decided to go part-time in my job as a speechwriter at the University of Wisconsin. We had decided it was time for me to focus on my freelance magazine writing and our three sons, all under the age of 9. I thought this pleasant life was the way it would always be, only it probably would get even better.

One night Dan was feeling ill. It was the second time in a couple weeks that he complained of stomach pains. It was hard to get Dan to go to the doctor, but he finally went, and the nightmare began.

The doctors found terminal colon cancer. Fourteen weeks later Dan was dead. My dear husband suffered horribly. He was in terrible pain, and there wasn't enough morphine in the world to take that pain away.

And then there was my own pain. I had no idea how I was going to get through this, let alone raise our three boys on my own. I even told Dan that I wished I were the one who was dying. I was afraid to survive.

Through his pain Dan said something to me that I couldn't comprehend at the time. I certainly didn't realize it was going to change the course of my life and career. "You are the right wife for this," he insisted. "In two years' time you will be so far from here. You are going to be a writer of merit."

"'Writer of merit'? What the heck does that mean?" I wondered.

It meant that after Dan died I made choices that inspired many people to tell me I was nuts.

I chose to write my first novel. Actually it felt like the novel chose me.

One night I had a dream and I woke up thinking, "This would make a good novel." I wrote down the dream, which had stories I had covered when I was a reporter. There was a theme of overwhelming grief and a mystery about what had happened to a child.

I shared the idea with a novelist friend and told her she should write the book.

"No, you should write this book," she challenged me.

"Me?" I countered. "How can I do that? I have three kids to raise. I'm broke. I'm writing little freelance articles for trade magazines like *Groundwater Age*. And on top of all that, I've never written a novel!"

My friend would not back down. "Those are really good excuses. Why don't you give it a try?"

That's when I realized I didn't have a choice. I had to try. Just about everyone told me I was crazy. People said, "Sell the house. Put everything in the stock market. Put the kids in day care at school. Get a full-time job."

That made me angry, and I said, "Enough! My kids and I have a hole in our hearts so big that it feels like life has driven a truck through us." I needed to prove to myself and my kids that there is life after death. Tragedy doesn't give you permission to give up on your dreams.

I wrote *The Deep End of the Ocean* to show my kids there was a reason to get out of bed. I was afraid they would have one parent who was dead and one who only had living organs. My boys deserved better than that.

It turns out I had a book agent because many years before I had written a nonfiction book about infertility and adoption. Infertility is another obstacle I faced—a story for another time.

I sent this book agent the first 60 pages I had written for the novel. Miraculously she sold *The Deep End of the Ocean* to the first publisher who looked at it. That was November. The publisher insisted the book be finished by December! I worked through the night, sometimes while the kids were asleep. But there was no doubt this choice of mine had costs for my already struggling family.

One of the kids' guidance counselors called me to inform me I wasn't behaving the way a widow should behave. "I see a woman obsessed with her career and not caring for her children. You need to get another job."

> I was afraid my kids would have one parent who was dead and one who only had living organs. My boys deserved better than that.

"Buddy, you should get another job," I informed him. "I'm here for my kids when they come home from school, which I wouldn't be if I went and got that full-time job."

Somehow we made it through those difficult months. The day I finished the novel, I was sitting at my desk, totally spent. I looked down at the calendar. It was two years to the day that Dan had died. I heard his words in my head, "In two years' time, you will be so far from here. You are going to be a writer of merit."

Even Dan couldn't have predicted what happened next. First, the book was a hit. Since I was new to the fiction world, I couldn't even appreciate some of the amazing things that were happening. My agent told me that *The Deep End of the Ocean* would be featured on the front page of *The New York Times Book Review*. "Is that good?" I had to ask. Apparently it is.

Then I started getting strange messages on my answering machine. "This is Oprah Winfrey. And I had to call to tell you that I've never enjoyed a book more." I erased the tape. I figured it was someone playing a joke on me.

She called twice more. Again I erased the messages. After the third call, my intern, a student at the university, said to me, "Uh, Jackie, I think this really is Oprah Winfrey! I think you should call her back."

So I called. "This is Jackie Mitchard. I've been erasing your messages." Oprah told me that she was calling as a fan just to tell me how much she enjoyed the book. But she also said, "I can't have you on the show because I don't do fiction."

Oprah must have had a change of heart because two weeks later she called back and said, "I've decided to start the world's largest book club and I'm going to start with your book."

That's how my novel became Oprah's first book club selection. It was like waving a magic wand as *The Deep End of the Ocean* went on to sell a million copies. I've now published 14 books and believe I've lived up to Dan's prediction. I am, indeed, a writer of merit.

Here's the important thing: Even if that first book hadn't been published, even if Oprah hadn't picked it for her book club, it still was the right thing to write it and go after my dream, despite what everyone was telling me.

My advice: When the going gets tough, that's when you take the risks that you never thought you would take. Try something impossible for you, whether it's weightlifting, running, or painting.

I don't mean do something nutty like drugs. But do take out your hidden dreams. Life is a terminal condition. Your "Some day" is right now. Go ahead and eat life alive.

Jacquelyn Mitchard's novel *Still Summer* was published in August 2007.

Prescription 4 Love

Ricky Durham,
website creator

There is someone out there for you to love.

I'm sure of it. I don't care if you have cancer, diabetes, a sexually transmitted disease, or any other physical challenge. I know because I've dedicated my life to helping others overcome the obstacle my late brother could not: finding love.

I live every day with the memory of my beloved younger brother, Keith. We were always very good friends, close in age, and always hung out together.

I have to be honest: He was much better looking than I am. I can remember going to an amusement park at the beach. He and a friend were walking about 30 or 40 feet in front of me. The girls would pass him and do a double take because he was so good looking.

Unfortunately for Keith what he had in abundance in the looks department did not translate into good health. As the years went by, it was clear there was something wrong with him. He kept losing weight, getting skinnier and skinnier. He burped a lot even when he hadn't been drinking soda or anything carbonated. I thought there was something wrong even before doctors diagnosed him.

It turned out that Keith had Crohn's disease, a chronic disease that causes inflammation of the digestive tract. It's a form of irritable bowel disease (IBD). About a half million people in North America suffer from Crohn's, and it really does involve suffering. For my brother, it meant terrible bouts of diarrhea and many hours in the bathroom.

As time went on Keith had multiple operations. Each time, the doctors cut out more and more of his colon. Finally he had to have a colostomy bag. That bag actually helped him out a lot because it meant he didn't have to spend endless hours in the bathroom. So for his last five years, he regained a bit of his life back.

Once Keith started feeling better, he was ready to get out of the house and start meeting new people. That's when things became difficult. He would meet people and hit it off. But then he would have a hard time telling women that he had a colostomy bag.

I mean, when do you tell someone you have a colostomy bag? Do you tell her on the first date? The second date? After two months? He could never figure out how to approach that subject at all.

My heart broke for him. Someone as great as my brother deserved to share his life with someone, bag or no bag. That's when I got the inspiration.

I thought, "What if he could meet someone who had the same condition or who also had a colostomy bag? Then there's nothing to disclose. You just move on to the next stages of the relationship from there."

Regular online dating services don't cater to that population. That's how I dreamed up Prescription4Love.com. Keith was very excited about the idea of an online dating service for people with special conditions. Unfortunately he died before I could get it up and running.

I miss him so much now that he's gone. I can't say that time has healed the pain. But I have been able to channel the grief into helping others find love.

I set up the website so that people can include their condition or physical challenge in their profile. Everyone knows up front, so there is nothing to hide.

I originally had Crohn's patients in mind when I launched Prescription4Love. Then this project quickly took off. I knew someone with diabetes who wanted a category. I knew someone who is deaf. Requests kept coming to include other categories. Eventually I launched with 11 conditions, but soon folks started writing in. "Why don't you add heart disease? What about fibromyalgia?" So I keep a running tab and add as I go. It's now up to 22 categories.

Even though my brother isn't here, this site is for him and others who have specific health conditions who want to improve their lives through love or friendship.

The site works like many other online dating services. It's simple. You pick a screen name, tell a little about yourself, such as your gender, age, hobbies, and where you live. But with Prescription4Love.com, you also click on which conditions you have. That way anyone who is interested in you knows up front.

I like helping people who are lonely because of their condition. I want to see them go on the site and find someone.

I love the feedback. I received the nicest email from a young woman in New York City who has cancer. She describes herself as "living with cancer." But she says every time she mentions this on a date, the guy will run for the hills. She wrote that it's such a relief to be able to be herself and tell her whole story without worrying about scaring someone else away. I love it when that happens.

> I like helping people who are lonely because of their health condition. I want to see them go on the site and find someone.

I can't say that there have been any marriages yet, but there are certainly some couples. I'm happy even when I just set up some friendships and members find they aren't quite as lonely anymore. You can no longer blame your physical condition for loneliness. There's a place where you can be you, condition and all.

I launched the website in February 2006. So far I haven't been charging for folks to use the site. I'm able to do that thanks to some generous financial support from my family, which also sees this as a tribute to Keith. Soon I will have to charge a small fee. When I do, I will donate a portion of that money to a charity for each of the conditions I feature.

I'm glad I had the chance to tell Keith about this before he died. I really wish he were here to use the site. And I'd love to tell him about all the big developments. I'm hoping he's looking down, saying, "I see it! I'm proud of you!"

In that way Prescription4Love.com has made another match of sorts. It's matched me with a positive place where I can pour my grief. I loved my brother so much and I miss him every day. I know he wouldn't want me sitting around feeling sad all the time. Making matches and giving others the opportunity to love has turned out to be my prescription for healing.

You can see more at prescription4love.com.

Shoulders to the Sky

Greg Rice,
Guinness World Records record holder

You might hear stories of someone losing his other half, but none like mine. My identical twin brother, John, was truly my other half. At 2 feet 10 inches tall we were in *Guinness World Records* for being the smallest living twins. Now there is no "we." Our journey has led me to do something significant on my own.

Our challenges started at the beginning. Sure, I often joked that we were "wombmates." But when we came into the world on December 3, 1951, no one was laughing. Our birth parents abandoned us at the hospital.

Thank goodness for our wonderful foster parents, who raised us. Although they weren't people of means, they instilled in us the sense that a person's real worth isn't measured from the top of your head to the bottom of your feet, rather from your shoulders to the sky! Our mother laid the foundation for what would become our motto: "Think big!"

It was a good thing we had that because we never topped 3 feet, and for most of our lives it was just the two of us against the world. Before we finished high school, both of our foster parents died. But we still had each other.

The best way I can describe how close John and I were comes from an act on the old *Ed Sullivan Show*. John and I knew how to spin each other's plates. I remember watching the Sullivan show when we were kids, and there was a performer who could spin a lot of plates on sticks. I remember being amazed at how he'd get several plates spinning; then when one would begin to wobble, he would spin it some more, then move to another one that was starting to wobble.

John and I worked like that throughout our lives. If one began to wobble, the other would instinctively know to spin the situation and straighten it out. We sure did a lot of spinning. Together we overcame the obstacle of our height to build a flourishing real estate career. We were local celebrities in Palm Beach County, Florida, doing TV commercials. We also spent countless hours as civic boosters, leading parades and speaking at schools.

With everything that we had faced and conquered, I can't say I was overly worried in November 2005 when John broke his leg. The break required surgery, but it was a routine procedure. It never occurred to me that he wouldn't leave that hospital alive.

People talk about your life flashing before you at the end of life. As I walked into the hospital recovery room and saw John's lifeless body lying there, I saw both of our lives flash before my eyes. I remembered in school during recess when the kids picked teams for kickball or red rover. It always seemed that the fast, athletic kids were chosen first. At our small size John and I clearly were not those fast-kid types. No, we were the slowest, even though we wanted to be picked so badly in the first group. We were almost always the last chosen.

Now, once again, I'm the last chosen.

I was 53 years old, and for the first time in my life I would have to go on without my business partner, my fiercest competitor, my best friend, my plate spinner. My challenge now has been making a new life without my identical twin brother.

I've gone over in my mind a thousand times, "Why did it have to happen?" I still can't answer it. But I've discovered that having all the answers isn't necessary for having a great life.

John and I had given thousands of motivational speeches. I realized that losing my brother was the ultimate test and opportunity to walk my talk. I look around and see that there are other people depending on me to spin their plates now. My son, my family, my business associates, my closest friends. How will I do that? I can't completely answer that yet. My whole life I've been half of the famous Rice Brothers. Well, the Rice Brothers are no more. What's my new identity? I'm still discovering that, and I know it will be very different from who I was for my first 53 years.

One thing I've learned is about the pain of loss. When it is fresh and raw, there is nothing that can lessen the pain or stop the hurt. You'd love to be able to reach those depths and make it better. It's impossible.

It is possible, however, that time brings space and opportunity. The space allows so many wonderful memories to seep in. If I'm riding in the car and I hear something or see something that John and I would have done together, just that thought spins my plate a little bit. Life should be about celebrating the positive and wonderful things that happen to us every day. Nobody ever happened upon a better brother than John.

> There's nothing like focusing on helping someone else to ease the pressure of your own pain.

The opportunity I see is to help others. It might be something as simple as being there for someone facing his or her own loss. There's nothing like consciously focusing on helping someone else to ease the pressure of your own pain.

John will always be a part of my life, and if he were here, I'd bet he would give you the same advice I give you: The people in your life are the most important thing. Any success you have, no matter how independent you think you are, involves other people. Value them because they make up the fabric of your life. And remember too that you are the fabric in someone else's life. You're valuable to other people in ways far beyond what you may know. Spend some time thinking about how you can contribute to others' lives, then take action. Speak up! Spin their plate.

And don't forget what my mama said: Success is measured from your shoulders to the sky. Think big!

Kate's Club

Kate Atwood,
founder of a grief support community center

I'm not a psychologist or a millionaire. I'm only in my twenties. But I have what it takes to start a special place for kids who have lost a parent or sibling. I simply created the place I wish I'd had after I lost my own mother to breast cancer when I was 12 years old.

I remember my mother, Audrey, as a great mom. She was a teacher, a job she chose so that she could always be available for my brother and me whether we were in school, taking dance classes, or participating in sports. With my father and brother, we made a perfect family of four.

Mom was first diagnosed with breast cancer when I was 6 years old. My parents shared this with us, but to a 6-year-old child those words don't really mean anything. I have a lot of respect for both my parents because even though I can now look back and see that my mother's disease was progressing, they didn't let that intrude on my childhood.

That also meant that it came as quite a shock when she died. I was in the middle of Mrs. Kerewich's social studies class when the call came over the intercom, paging me to come to the school office. I knew right away that Mom was gone. Just the night before I had rushed home from my Little League softball game to jump into my mom's arms, only to find an empty bed. She had gone to the hospital for the last time.

I remember being at the hospital and feeling totally devastated. As an adult I now know that it doesn't matter whether it's a prolonged illness or a car accident that takes your parent. One day your parent is there; the next, she isn't. It's about as black and white as you can get.

Twelve is a tough time for a girl to lose her mom—I was going through adolescence without Mom there to explain all the changes. Her death also came at a time when I was desperate to fit in with the other kids. Since I was the only one I knew whose mom had died, fitting in seemed even harder.

My dad and brother did the best they could, but they were dealing with loss too; my brother lost his mother and my father lost his wife. Suddenly this family unit that had been glued together emotionally by one person had lost its glue. Looking back I can see we all floundered through those years. I turned in one direction, my father another, and my brother yet another, not from an absence of love but rather from the presence of sadness, grief, and guilt.

> Working with kids at a bereavement camp made me realize how much I had missed this kind of support.

To look at me, though, you would have thought I was doing fine. And on paper I was. I did well in school, excelled in sports. I went to college and after graduation started a career in sports marketing. I believed that if everything looked good on paper, then everyone around me would think I was OK.

But grief is not visible, and everything was not OK. The dam began to break in my first year in college when suddenly I was in a new environment. Six years of sadness came pouring out. Fortunately I found a camp for bereaved children where I could volunteer. Immediately I found working with younger kids at this camp to be comforting, and it helped to be with others who had experienced the same kind of loss I had. That experience also made me realize how much I had missed this kind of support and camaraderie during my own childhood. That's where the seeds were planted for Kate's Club, although I didn't see it at the time. I was too focused on graduating from college and starting my career.

Working in sports marketing comes with some nice perks, including getting free tickets to sporting events. I found myself organizing little outings for kids I met who had just lost a parent. As I saw how much fun and how beneficial those outings were, I became inspired to take it to the next step.

That's how Kate's Club was born. A lot of people probably wondered what I was doing. I was only 24, walking away from a promising career in sports marketing to start a nonprofit, something I knew nothing about and certainly didn't have the deep pockets to fund. But I did have the experience of being one of those grieving kids, and I had the passion to create a resource unlike any other.

Kate's Club is a clubhouse where kids find a community of support after they've lost a parent or sibling. I like to say that we're about 80 percent youth development, 20 percent grief support.

In a lot of ways, we are countercultural at Kate's Club. There are no victims here, only survivors. We help these kids connect with each other while also connecting with their grief. And we help them reconnect with hope and opportunity and fun. Kate's Club offers our kids a world where it is OK to grieve.

This can surprise a lot of traditionalists in the grief support world. It also surprises a lot of the kids when they first arrive. They come expecting to be greeted by a matronly woman dressed in black—the image they associate with death and grief counseling. Instead they meet me—upbeat, young, and dressed in pink.

I remember the first family I ever welcomed here. I walked into the room to meet three little girls whose father had just passed away. The youngest sister looked up at the oldest sister and said, "She doesn't look like I thought she would."

For more information visit katesclub.org.

Daryn's Takeaways

* *

Starting a grief camp was too big a project for Kate to handle at her age and experience level, so she asked herself, "If I keep breaking it down, what level can I handle?" She began by taking a few kids to sporting events. Now Kate's Club, a nationally recognized organization, serves 100 kids a month. What about you? Do you have a dream that seems bigger than your experience level? How could you scale it down to something you can manage?

Part 6

· ·

Finding the Perfect Niche: Creative Entrepreneurs

Free Shoes

Blake Mycoskie,
founder of TOMS Shoes

I refused to look at a map or ask for directions. That mistake cost me $1 million but changed the course of my life for the better.

It wasn't just anywhere that I refused to look at a map. It was on national television. In 2002 my sister, Paige, and I competed on Season 2 of *The Amazing Race*, the CBS reality show. We were doing really well right up until the last leg of the game. That's when we came to a juncture where we didn't know which way to go in the fast-paced race-around-the-world game. Paige wanted to pull out our map. No, I insisted that I knew the direction to go. We didn't need to look at a map or ask for directions. I wouldn't take "map" for an answer. We went with my guess, and it was the wrong direction. Paige and I ended up losing the race by 4 minutes!

It was painful to lose *The Amazing Race* by 4 minutes, especially when we had just spent 31 days racing around the world trying to win. I was bummed, big time. I decided to try to get over my disappointment by taking some time to go back to all these countries that I had spent about 10 minutes in. This time I would really immerse myself in the culture. I went back to Africa, and next I went to Belize. Then I headed farther south to Argentina. That's where my life changed forever.

My original plan for Argentina was fairly exotic. I wanted to learn how to become a polo player. I laugh about that now. For the first three weeks, I lived among the rich, the elite, and the privileged of that beautiful country. Polo players are as famous and popular in Argentina as NFL players are here in the United States, so you can imagine there were some celebrity perks as well.

My big discovery during that time was the *alpargata*. This is a type of shoe that has been worn by Argentinean farmers for hundreds of years. In the last 10 years, they've become kind of trendy in Buenos Aires: The polo players in training on the farms saw the farmers wearing the shoes and started wearing them too. Then the players' girlfriends started wearing them to the pool and cafes. *Alpargatas* happen to be super comfortable, and I also found myself wearing them all the time.

As my friends and I drove from Buenos Aires to polo fields in nearby towns, I started to notice something else—poverty unlike anything I had ever seen—people living in trash dumps, people who don't have any shoes and who have cuts and infections because they have to walk over rocks to get to fresh water.

I believe that by giving away free shoes, we get so many people excited about what we're doing, they'll tell everyone they know.

I grew up in a middle-class family in Texas. I'd never really seen that level of poverty, so when I saw it for the first time it really affected me. I decided I wasn't going to come all the way to Argentina just for four weeks of playing polo. So when the polo gig was over, I decided to spend a week volunteering in one of the local impoverished towns. That's where I first encountered children without any shoes. And it was during that week that I had my "Aha!" epiphany moment.

I would start a shoe company with shoes styled after the *alpargata*. For every pair of shoes sold, the company would hand-deliver a pair to a child in need. I decided to call the company TOMS Shoes, "TOMS" as in providing shoes for tomorrow.

Now keep in mind, I knew *nothing* about having a shoe company whatsoever. And I didn't know anything about fashion either. How clueless was I? When I got back to the United States, I showed my shoes to some girls. They said, "Oh, these would look really good with skinny jeans!" So I spent the next week going from store to store, looking for a brand called "Skinny Jeans." Someone finally clued me in that it was actually a style of jeans, not a brand of jeans!

I can give you 20 more stories about the times I put my foot in my mouth about shoes and fashion. But each time I learned more and more. I figured out enough to modify the shoes for a North American market. The original shoe had a rope sole and a canvas upper. I wanted it to be more durable, so I replaced the rope with a rubber sole. Then I put in a leather insole so people can wear them without socks and their feet won't sweat or get stinky. And I produced them in many bright, fashionable colors and patterns.

Most people told me that my idea to give away free shoes was crazy. It definitely did not get me any support from my financial friends when I started. That's why I bootstrapped it and financed the whole company myself.

The usual reaction was "Well, that's nice if you want to start a nonprofit, but if you're going to try to start a company, it makes no sense to give one pair away for every pair that you sell."

This concept, though, is really based on my belief that by giving away the free shoes, we create so much good in the world and get so many people excited about what we're doing that they're going to feel compelled to tell everyone they know. The word of mouth means we don't have to spend all that money on advertising and marketing that most shoe companies have to spend.

My dreams and vision are coming true. So far TOMS has sold tens of thousands of shoes around the world. That means, yes, we've also given away that many shoes.

The first shoe drop was back in Argentina. It was absolutely amazing! It was the greatest experience of my life. I can hardly express the feeling of putting a new pair of shoes on a child for the first time in his life and seeing him run off and play or show his mom and dad; or telling a child through a translator how she's now able to go to school because she finally has a pair of shoes. It touches me on the deepest level, a level where I had never been touched before.

It's funny when I think back on losing *The Amazing Race*. It was completely my fault and I have apologized profusely to my sister. I figure I probably owe her a half million bucks! But I also know if we had won the competition, I wouldn't be doing this. I probably would have taken my million and bought real estate and become a developer. I'm very thankful that something that was devastating at the time turned out to be a big blessing. I find that happens regularly in my life.

Finally, for all those who criticize men for not looking at a map or asking for directions, I have to say this time that stubborn move paid off—that mistake ended up pointing my life in exactly the best direction I ever could have taken.

For more information go to tomsshoes.com.

Daryn's Takeaways

. . . .

Sorry, guys, the moral of this story is not that you shouldn't ask for directions! Rather it's a wonderful example that some of life's big disappointments really set us up for greatness.

The Birth of the Zingo Nation

PX Head,
president of Zingo

I was at the wheel in a drunk driving accident

that took the life of one of my best friends, Benjamin Hawkins. I could be in prison, but I received an amazing second chance from the most surprising place.

Let me take you back to the night I made the worst choice of my life: June 11, 2004. My friends and I were home on break from the University of Georgia. It was a weekend night in Atlanta. No one had to work the next day, so we met up for happy hour. We had several cocktails through the night together and had a great time. I don't know how much I had to drink, but it was certainly more than the legal limit.

Still, when it was time to call it a night, I got behind the wheel. Four buddies piled in. Benjamin sat behind me in the passenger seat. Within just blocks of my house, I made a turn and lost control of the car. I don't remember clearly how it all happened, but I began swerving, overcorrecting the steering wheel. I completely lost control of the car. We slammed broadside into a telephone pole, the impact hitting right behind me on the passenger door where Benjamin was sitting. He was killed instantly.

What an incredible loss. Benjamin Hawkins was the total package:

witty, charming, intelligent, charismatic, and a straight-A student. Everyone liked him. He was one of the good guys out there. And because of my accident, he was gone.

I woke up in the hospital handcuffed to the bed. I was totally confused and couldn't figure out what was going on. There was a police officer there. He said, "Do you know Benjamin Hawkins?"

I said, "Yes."

He said, "He was killed in your car accident tonight. You're under arrest." At that point my whole world stopped. One of my best friends was dead, and I was facing vehicular manslaughter charges and 10 years in prison.

> My best friend was dead, and I was facing vehicular manslaughter charges and 10 years in prison.

But before I faced my legal fate, I had to face Benjamin's family. Two days later my parents drove me down to Benjamin's hometown of Macon, Georgia. As I went up to his family's front door, I had no idea what I would say. I was terrified beyond words. What would happen?

Nothing could have prepared me for what was about to occur. Benjamin's mother opened the door and grabbed me and hugged me. We both started crying, and I just kept saying, "I'm sorry. I'm sorry."

The most amazing thing happened that day: Benjamin's family told me that they forgave me. And they took their actions a step further. They wrote letters to the district attorney and the judge saying that they had forgiven me, that they didn't hold any ill will toward me, and that they didn't want to see me go to prison!

It was the most amazing example of forgiveness, faith, and grace I'd ever experienced. I could have been convicted of a felony and sent to prison for 10 years. Instead I pled guilty to vehicular homicide and was sentenced to 30 days in county jail and 10 years' probation.

At the end of the court proceeding, the prosecuting attorney came over, shook my hand, and said, "You just got back the best 10 years of your life. Go do something with them."

First, though, I had to do the 30 days in Fulton County's overcrowded jail. That was a nightmare. I didn't know if I would survive, much less what I was going to do when I was released.

There were many harsh, soul-searching days as I wondered what would become of me. I thought I had a bright future working as an investment banker or perhaps an investor or hedge fund manager. My vehicular homicide conviction now removed those career options completely. I had no idea what to do. My dream was over. I was just hoping to find anything to do when I was released.

About a month after getting out of jail, I heard about a new business forming in my hometown of Atlanta. Zingo turned out to be my second chance.

Zingo is a designated-driver service with a twist: Drivers take you home in your own car. Most people drink and drive in the first place because they want to have their car in the morning for work or for errands. That's why they don't call a cab or ask a buddy for a ride home.

That's why people love Zingo: It's the ultimate convenience! Party as much as you want, then have someone drive you home in your car.

How does Zingo do that? By using a special Italian motorbike, the Di Blasi, that folds up in two seconds and can be put into a canvas bag. All you have to do is call Zingo; a driver rides to you on the motorbike, collapses the bike, and puts it in the back of your car. You hand over the keys; the driver gets behind the wheel, takes you home, pops open the motorbike, and drives off into the night. Zingo does it all for about the same price of a cab ride.

I saw Zingo and was instantly smitten. I could see the value of giving people an easy option to call for a driver rather than endangering the lives of dozens of people by trying to drive home drunk. I was so smitten that I bought into the company and now serve as president.

I'm absolutely certain that we've saved thousands of lives, with thousands more to come. My real goal is to have Zingo running all across the country. I see a Zingo nation!

As you can imagine, when you're servicing the bar crowd and building a new business, the hours are crazy. This is the last thing I thought I would be doing with my college degree.

But I truly feel like I'm making good on that amazing second chance. Nothing will ever bring Benjamin back or repair the pain that the accident caused his family. But if I can get Zingo running across the country and prevent just one family from getting a phone call like the

Hawkinses did, then all the hard work will be worth it.

Speaking of Benjamin's family, at first I purposely didn't share with them what I was doing. I didn't want to cause them any more pain or remind them of that awful time. They had already given me an amazing second chance. I didn't think it was also their job to cheer me on.

I found out recently that his parents know exactly what I'm doing, and they're very pleased. They saw a video about Zingo and are spreading the word. Now some of their friends are considering starting a Zingo franchise in Benjamin's hometown. That makes me feel better than I can ever describe.

I don't know where Benjamin's family found the strength to give me a second chance. I do know that each time a Zingo driver heads out to get someone home safely, it's a tribute to my friend, giving both our lives meaning and purpose, even as his life was way too short.

For more information go to callzingo.com.

Smooth Mooove

Adrienne Simpson,
founder and president of
Smooth Mooove Senior Relocation Services

Getting laid off from my cushy corporate executive job is one of the best things that ever happened to me. Thousands face downsizing every year. I'm here to tell you, it can lead to a larger life with more meaning and purpose than you ever imagined.

I'm clear on this. I was a successful executive, focused, committed, and all the other things we learn in school that we need to be to get ahead. And I loved the life of an important job, travel, and an expense account. You can imagine my surprise then when I was downsized out of corporate leadership positions, not once but twice!

The first time, I had worked myself up over the course of 20 years from the position of clerk-typist to director of operations for a national health insurance company and was in charge of 300 people. I loved my people and my people loved me. Then the layoff notice came.

One thing they don't teach you in executive school is how to pick yourself up from the smoking crater that used to be your career. I was left to my own devices to figure that one out.

At that time I lived with my husband and daughter in Detroit. My job loss was an utter shock, but I figured I'd find another job quickly. Wrong!

My prospects were bleak, and to make matters worse my husband decided to divorce me.

I had to get out of town. So I packed my daughter in the car and headed to anywhere, which happened to be Atlanta. We were going to have girl power and take on anything that came our way.

I was able to get a sales rep job in Atlanta, and in no time I was the top salesperson in the nation for another major health care corporation. When the director of operations job opened, I grabbed it and quickly turned the whole corporation around. But wouldn't you know it, a few years later I was downsized again!

> I didn't want to move past the life of a corporate executive, but life came and moved me along to a better place.

This time I hit the wall hard. I went from the executive life, perks, and income to being unemployed—again. I was very depressed and remember many days sending my daughter off to school, then going back to bed. I did this not for days but for months. I felt that my worth to a huge degree was dependent on what I did. Since I was doing nothing, I was nothing in my own eyes. So much for girl power. Instead I felt like a meek little squeak. I knew I was finished.

Then a simple family event began to change my world. It started with my wonderful mother. Mom had moved to Atlanta to help me with my daughter as I rebuilt my life as a single mother. But once my daughter grew older, Mom decided her work here was done and she wanted to move back home to Michigan. She wanted help with the move, and since I was just sitting around depressed, doing nothing, I looked like the obvious choice.

I figured I'd just look up a seniors' moving service and it would do it all. I needed somebody to help me sort, clean, and pack and do it with a sensitive touch. News flash—there was no such service. I had to do it myself.

I learned a lot with my mom's move. Moving seniors can involve many steps. It's not just the packing and moving. There are also clearing, sorting, organizing, transporting, unpacking, estate sales, antique appraisal, donations, heirloom delivery, cleaning, and primping the house for its next life. There's also counseling older folks who can be very uncomfortable with change.

While I was doing all this work, my mother was going to church, telling all her friends, "I'm moving and I don't have to lift a finger. My daughter is doing everything!"

Once Mom was settled back in Michigan, those same friends started calling me, saying they needed help. Without even realizing it I started my new business and new life. Smooth Mooove is the moving company that specializes in moving seniors.

It took all the money I could muster from severance, unemployment, savings, retirement, and just plain scraping to buy a 14-foot box truck to launch the company. But the business exploded! Even without advertising, the business has grown 20 to 35 percent each year. I now have 12 to 20 people on my payroll at any time, depending on how many moves we're handling.

Even better, I found my life purpose. Moving seniors is a very tender responsibility. It can be traumatic for people who are leaving and grieving for the home they've lived in for most of their adult lives. If their grown children have careers and families of their own and can't be on hand to help, seniors can feel overwhelmed and admit, "I can't do this. I need some help." Smooth Mooove is that help.

When you ask regular movers to unpack, they take everything out of the box and leave it on the floor. We put everything where it is supposed to be. In fact we don't even call it unpacking. We call it resettling.

We set up the display of family pictures; we make sure the person knows where the television remote is. One of our trademark touches is to make the bed. We like to make sure that when we leave our clients, they can sleep, shower, and have a meal. We treat each client as if he or she were our own grandparent.

Of course, there were many lessons to learn in creating my first company. I had the customer service skills down from my corporate life, but being a mover, counselor, adviser, truck driver, confidante, motivator, and surrogate child was all new to me.

I also learned from all the elderly. For instance, it's important to involve them in the process and keep them involved as much as possible. Also I recommend giving a newly widowed person six to nine months to grieve and adjust to the loss of a spouse before encouraging a move. Rushing elderly people to suit your schedule is a bad policy. If they refuse to move but staying put isn't a viable option, get pastors and doctors involved; advice coming from these respected figures is more likely to be accepted.

Maybe it's just part of human nature. Most of us don't like to move. I know I didn't want to move past the life of a corporate executive. Life came and moved me along to a better place. I like to think I'm doing the same for my senior clients, moving them to a place and surroundings that will actually serve them better.

I wouldn't sell this business for $20 million! I get more pleasure than I can say providing our seniors with dignity, respect, and understanding support. If I can help take one obstacle out of their lives, I consider it a Smooth Mooove.

For more information go to wemoveseniors.com.

Daryn's Takeaways

I love the way Adrienne Simpson has reinvented herself. Reinvention is really the chapter almost all of us eventually face. The opportunity could result from a corporate layoff, a divorce, or finding yourself with an empty nest once the kids grow up.

Eventually we each will face the time when the thing we did, the thing that defined us, goes away. Then what? It's time to reinvent.

It can either be the most amazing opportunity to build an even more meaningful life or it can beat you. It's a choice.

The Do-Good Junkie

James Burgett,
recovering drug addict, computer and people recycler

I've been homeless. I've been hooked on heroin and speed.
But on the way to finding new purpose in my life, I've found a new thing to
be hooked on: recycling computers—and people society has given up on.

If you look at my life beginning with my dysfunctional childhood,
you could easily call me a bipolar, drug-abusing lunatic with a history of
violence. I've become much more self-aware and now have better coping
mechanisms as an adult. My safety net has been finding that it's cool to be
addicted to helping people.

I now run the Alameda County Computer Resource Center. I have a
building full of thrown-away people taking thrown-away stuff and turning
it into something everybody wants: computers.

My challenges started with a childhood that was severely dysfunctional
by any standards. I bounced around quite a bit. By the time I was 17, I
had lived in more than 17 different houses. My parents divorced when
I was young. I lived mainly with my mother and a series of stepfathers,
including one who beat me.

I tried life with my father, which wasn't much better. At one time he
was a successful software engineer. By the time I lived with him and my
stepmother, he was involved in a cult and battling mental illness.

You can see why by my midteens I was basically on my own. Perhaps you might understand the self-image problems and pain I battled every day. Drugs were the easy answer. By the time I was 17, I was hard core into heroin and speed. That went on in one form or another for many years.

Along the way there were sparks of hope and possibility. The first bright light was a chance to work as a seasonal firefighter with the California Conservation Corps. For the first time in my life, I had a great self-image. Everyone loves firefighters! Little old ladies will hike three miles in the middle of the night to give firefighters a plate of cookies. It was great to belong to something so positive.

> It got to a point where I knew I had to make a choice. The opportunity to do good in the world made the difference.

That made the summers fantastic. I had no need or desire to do drugs. But come winter I would fall back into being really stupid again and doing more drugs.

This is about the time I started tinkering with computers. My formal education ended around eighth grade, but my dad had exposed me to computers early, so I've always been very comfortable around them. Contrary to what most people believe, computers don't explode when you try to repair them. There are no more than 10 components, and no component will let you connect it to the wrong spot unless you have really big biceps and a small forehead.

I began getting my first taste of recycling when I worked with the Marin Conservation Corps. I rode on its recycling trucks as the person who would sort and throw stuff into the bins.

On a darker note, I also started pulling discarded computers out of trash bins. I would salvage three or four computers in various states of repair. From those I could turn out two or three fully functioning machines, sell them, and use the proceeds to buy drugs.

Somehow I was good enough at this to start a little business called Counterculture Computers. My motto was "No Suit. No Tie. No Bull."

One day I received a call from a day care center saying it had just received a big donation of used computers but needed them fixed. The deal was I would fix up the best ones for the day care center for free and keep the rest of the parts for my own business.

Somewhere along the way more requests like this came in. I had no intention at that point of going into the do-good business. I thought I would just help out the folks on that short list and shut it down.

But one of the local community papers did a story in the Sunday edition about my project at the day care center. The next morning I was awakened by a call from a software company. The representative said he had read about me in the paper, liked what he saw, and asked if I wanted a couple hundred used computers.

I accepted, not realizing the scale of what I was taking on. My wife and I were living in a two-room bungalow at the time, and that's where I worked on the computers too. It got to the point where we had to create small pathways to get to every part of the two rooms.

My wife is an incredibly patient woman, but even she had had it at this point. She told me I had to go do something real with all this stuff.

I called around Marin County looking for a storage company that would work with me, one that would let me replace the usual lightbulb with a socket adapter so I could work in the space. Storage companies don't like to pay for more electricity, but I finally found one that would. That storage company basically subsidized my operation by paying for the electricity.

Suddenly I had a nonprofit with a small staff helping people who needed computers but couldn't afford them. More newspaper stories came out. More donations started showing up. We had to keep renting bigger storage units.

The company finally burst at the seams, and I realized we needed to take the huge step of renting industrial space. I went for 1,000 square feet and called it The Barn because I thought that was huge! The first time I walked in I said, "We'll never fill this space." Two weeks later we were already negotiating for more space in the building.

Things continued to explode. The company now had a county recycling contract. The extra revenue and materials meant rebuilding even more computers to give away.

There was just one hitch. I still wasn't completely clean and off drugs. From time to time I would go off and have some serious binges.

It finally got to a point where I knew I had to make a choice.

The opportunity to do good in the world made the difference. I have never been able to get clean for my own sake. I also have no interest in God or religion. But making a difference in people's lives is bigger than I am. I could see it. It's now and it's real. I can demonstrate that it's beneficial to the people around me.

Because of that I finally had no need to do drugs. That was 1998. I've been clean ever since.

The Alameda County Computer Resource Center is now one of the largest nonprofit computer recycle centers in the United States.

We take in 250,000 pounds of discarded electronics every month. That is 3 million pounds a year of waste that isn't going into a landfill. From that we rebuild and give away at least 12 computers every week.

The machines go to schools, nonprofits, underprivileged homes, disabled individuals, and developing countries. We'll give computers to anyone who can come up with a good reason to need one.

We've placed computers on every continent. Yes, I can say every continent since I gave computers to a Chilean expedition that was exploring Antarctica.

I don't just recycle computers. I recycle people. I hire almost exclusively from drug treatment centers, prison work-release programs, and psychiatric work-release programs.

Where some might see what they consider broken people, I see heroes. We understand each other and develop a tribe mentality. We do things other people think are impossible and we do it with garbage.

The man who runs my warehouse has nine felony convictions. In most places no one would trust him with a burned-out match. He's doing a remarkable job. Another guy has a history of cocaine addiction and is so tied up in various bureaucracies that I can't pay him any more money or he'll lose his housing. He comes here every day anyway and volunteers on the days he's not allowed to work. The guy who handles all of our community collection field events hears voices. He's the best guy I've ever had for this job. When you know that you periodically receive false data in your head, you develop a talent for being focused and keeping track of details. If I sit down with him and tell him what needs to be done point by point, it will be done perfectly every time.

Each of the 18 men and women on my staff now has the same thing going that I do. Each gets up in the morning because this is the best thing he or she can be doing.

That would be my best advice to people who are battling addictions. Find something to do. Find something you want to get behind. It doesn't matter what you do as long as it's something that helps you paint a new self-image so that when you look in the mirror, you see someone more than a hurting drug user. It's easier if it's something you feel is doing good in the world.

I never stopped being an addict. But now I'm addicted to doing good.

You can learn about the recycled computers and reclaimed lives at the Alameda County Computer Resource Center at accrc.org.

Daryn's Takeaways

James' story and advice remind me of something a friend said to me during a time when I was particularly down. "Go be of service," she said.

She wasn't going to spend time trying to make me feel better or convince me that things weren't bad. But she understood a certain law of emotional physics. You can't spend as much energy feeling "woe is me" about yourself and your problems when you are focused on helping someone else.

Go volunteer somewhere and you'll find you've stopped your emotional spiral, at least for a while. And as James pointed out, you'll get a different kind of high that comes from helping others. You will have put some good in the world, which is far more helpful to the big picture than sitting around feeling sorry for yourself.

Where could you go today to volunteer some of your time?

Making Money for Fun

Cameron Johnson,
millionaire at 15

Like a lot of people, I had big dreams of making millions of dollars. There was one big obstacle that most people would see in me when I started out: I was just a kid. I started going after my dream when I was 8 years old. Where other people see obstacles, I see adventure.

I'm 23 years old now. That means I've been chasing my big business dreams for 15 years!

I was only 8 years old when I sent my first official business letter to Donald Trump. I'd watched *Home Alone 2, Lost in New York* with Macaulay Culkin and wanted to do everything he'd done. Donald Trump had a cameo appearance in the movie because it was filmed at The Plaza in New York. So I begged my parents to take me to New York City.

My parents were wise and made a deal with me. They said, "If you get straight A's, we'll take you to New York City this summer." I was in fourth grade at the time, so getting A's was fairly easy. Since my parents always did what they said they'd do, I knew I was going to New York City.

What my parents didn't know was that I really wanted to see the suite that was filmed in the movie. I wasn't sure how to go about doing that, so I wrote a letter to Donald Trump and addressed it to "Donald Trump, Trump Plaza, New York City."

The letter said, "Dear Mr. Trump, my name is Cameron Johnson. I'm 8 years old. I'm from Roanoke, Virginia. You probably don't know who I am because I'm just a kid..." And I told him details about myself and when my family was going to arrive. I had no idea if it would ever get to him. In fact I never heard back. Oh, well.

When we checked into the hotel, the receptionist turned to us and said, "You must be Cameron!" My mom totally freaked out.

The receptionist continued by saying, "Mr. Trump received your letter and he's sorry he couldn't meet you personally, but he understands that you wanted to see the suite where the movie was filmed. He's actually arranged for your family to stay in the suite the entire time you're here. He's also arranged for you to have the Talk Boy Recorder that Macaulay Culkin used in the movie, and he has arranged for you to have a private tour of FAO Schwarz tomorrow morning. You'll have a gift basket awaiting you with cookies and an I Love New York T-shirt."

He left me a signed business card, and the shock of it all was huge. My mom was really mad at me at first. But she got over it.

The next day at FAO Schwarz, I told my dad I needed a business card to give back to Mr. Trump. So I had business cards made with my name, Cameron Johnson; my home address; and at the suggestion of my dad, "entrepreneur" in bold letters. I didn't even know what that meant, but my dad said it would make a great impression. I left him a note when we checked out, along with one of my cards. I'll never forget that moment as long as I live.

I guess the term "entrepreneur" was a good choice because I was always selling stuff. Lemonade stands, fresh vegetables door-to-door. I loved all of it. I soon set my eye on getting a computer, not for video games like most kids but to sell more stuff.

I got my first computer when I was 12, and it changed my life almost immediately.

The computer had software that allowed you to print greeting cards, announcements, and even business cards! It had templates that you could use to customize your cards. My mom had a party coming up for the holidays, and I told her that for $15 I'd print up all her invitations.

A business was born. I stayed at it, doing cards and invitations for all my mom's friends and neighbors. In about two years I'd saved around

$4,000. I upgraded my computer and was set to expand my business when something brand new was born on the Internet: eBay.

By coincidence my 6-year-old sister had been collecting Beanie Babies. I offered to buy her whole collection for $100! To a kindergartner $100 is like a gazillion dollars, and she went crazy. I immediately got on eBay and sold them all within days for $1,000! $900 profit! For the record, I've since paid her back the $900 plus interest.

> I learned that obstacles are there only if you see them. If you look past them, things are much easier.

Things grew rapidly even though I had no idea what I was doing. I would just ask for whatever I wanted, and amazing things happened. For example, I was able to find a supplier for my Beanie Babies, and at the age of 14 I was ordering direct and selling direct. My mom got me a custodial checking account and a Visa check card. I thought I'd really arrived! I was taking and shipping 40 orders a day right out of my bedroom. To keep my expenses down, I used the free Priority Mail packaging from the post office and did all my ordering online. I was young but somehow I just stumbled along and figured it out.

I made $50,000 selling Beanie Babies that year. My dual life began. On one hand I was a normal kid with Boy Scouts, soccer, and homework. On the other I was the owner of a booming business. Things really took off when I started a free email service for kids. Ad revenue brought in the money. I started winning awards and worldwide recognition. But I swear I still felt like a normal 14-year-old.

Over the next couple of years, between school and athletics I ran an Internet operation that was making $15,000 a day in revenue. When I put out a press release about my success, it was picked up worldwide. And of all the crazy things, I became famous in Japan! Someone there wrote a book about me, a 15-year-old millionaire CEO sensation from America. When I'd travel there (with my parents), people would mob me. A Japanese company made me a board member and spent $1 million promoting me, setting up speaking tours and getting me extensive television coverage. One girl asked me to autograph her $600 Prada purse. I didn't know anything about that stuff, and my dad told me that my mom didn't even have one of those. I took out my Sharpie and wrote "Cameron Johnson" across it. She loved it, but my mom would have fainted if she had known I'd just signed a Prada.

Then I'd come back home and go back to being a normal high school kid. It was an amazing time, and much has come out of all those experiences. I have had so many wonderful experiences that have convinced me repeatedly that in life you just have to ask for what you want.

This isn't to say that there haven't been obstacles—well, obstacles as far as other people could see. Other people would see a kid trying to compete in an adult's world. Other people would see a kid trying to balance going back and forth between a grown-up world and a kid world.

But I learned something more important than business lessons with my early success. I learned that obstacles are there only if you see them. If you look past them, things are much easier.

I am now at the ripe old age of 23. I spend my time focusing on speaking worldwide to various groups on entrepreneurship, and I have several web-based businesses and a book titled *You Call the Shots*.

In many ways I'm still the little kid who sent off letters to Donald Trump. Every day I awake with a gleam in my eye, ready to ask the world for amazing things and watch what comes back.

My advice is focus on that spark, on your passion, and not on what other people look at and call obstacles.

You can learn more at cameronjohnson.com.

Daryn's Takeaways

. . . .

Cameron is like many of the people featured in this book. The hardest part about interviewing them was getting them to talk about problems and challenges. They simply don't see them. Hey, Cameron, what about the fact that you were just a kid? "I didn't think about it," he shrugged. He was having too much fun. It's a great lesson we can all learn from. This is not to say most of us won't face problems and challenges in going for our dreams. But I honestly believe that what you think about expands. Dwell on the problems and challenges, and they will become bigger. Focus on your dream, your vision, your passion, and that is what will expand and flourish.

Sweet Opportunity

Michele Hoskins,
single mother and entrepreneur

Becoming a divorced mother of three girls might not seem like the best time to make big business dreams and become an entrepreneur. Yet that's exactly what I did thanks to a recipe handed down from my great-great-great-grandmother, an emancipated slave.

I am the great-great-great-granddaughter of America Washington, a former slave who was freed in 1866. America stayed on to work for the Mississippi family who owned her and her mother. She was a talented cook looking for ways to please this family of picky eaters. Apparently someone in the family didn't like the taste of molasses. So America developed a syrup recipe made of churned butter, honey, and cream.

America had seven or eight children and handed down the recipe to her third daughter. I'm not sure why, but the family tradition was born. The honey cream syrup recipe was to be handed down to the third daughter of each generation.

It also became a wonderful part of my family's tradition. I can remember as a child going over to my grandmother and great-grandmother's house each Sunday. They would fix homemade waffles and that delicious syrup.

More than 120 years after America was emancipated, I found myself facing a different kind of freedom: divorce. I was a schoolteacher with three daughters to raise. This could be a daunting task.

But I was reading how the 1980s were supposed to be the decade of the woman. Women were emerging as the heads of companies, as CEOs. I thought, "Wow! I want to be a part of that!" I decided I was going to be an entrepreneur. Keep in mind, I had very little idea what that meant. I thought it meant being independent and in control of my own destiny. That was good enough for me.

In fact I decided to be a successful businesswoman before I even decided what my business would be. One morning it hit me, "America's syrup!" Everyone loved coming over to the family's house for Sunday breakfast. Surely customers would like to buy it as well!

The first challenge was getting my mother to give up the recipe. My mother had three children, but I was her only daughter, so technically she shouldn't hand it down to me. I convinced her that she was actually passing it down to my youngest daughter, who was the third girl. And I had the idea to make it into a business.

First I tried making a big batch of America's syrup on the stove and taking that around to local restaurants. This was pretty much a disaster because the syrup would separate and the restaurants told me it wouldn't work.

I certainly was discouraged but far from defeated. There were plenty of maple syrups on the store shelves, so I knew there had to be a way to make syrup properly; I just had to figure it out.

Finally with my mother's help we perfected the recipe, and a local Chicago company helped me with producing large batches commercially. The company also helped with designing labels and bottles.

That's where I hit another roadblock. There was no money to manufacture a large enough batch to sell. So I did what I had to—sold everything I had and moved in with my mother. My three daughters and I lived in her attic.

I had the right product, the right bottle, the right label, and the right copacker that would make the syrup for me. But I couldn't afford to have the company bottle it. So I set up in my mother's basement, using a funnel to pour the syrup into each individual bottle, pasting on the labels by hand, and putting the bottles in a box ready to go around to local merchants.

No doubt people thought I was a little crazy. "Oh, yeah," they'd say. "She's the lady down in the basement making syrup. Leave her alone. She's lost her mind."

I saw myself as determined. I went around to local shops and made a deal with them. I asked them to put the syrup on their shelves. If it sold I would come back and fill out the invoice. If it didn't I would come back in 30 days and take it back.

I had no advertising or marketing budget, but I knew I had to create an illusion of movement. So I would come back to those stores and buy a few bottles myself. Then I would send a girlfriend in to buy a bottle. The stores started thinking Michele's syrup was flying off the shelves! And they ordered more.

> Anything the mind can conceive can be made manifest through hard work, perseverance, and faith.

A couple of big breaks put me on the map. First the buyer at Jewel Supermarket agreed to put me in all his stores if his grandson liked the product. Of course, his grandson did. The big order meant I could now afford to have my syrup bottled at the copacker. I finally came out of the basement!

That level of success was fine for a time, but I had bigger plans. I wanted national exposure. I set my sights on Denny's. This was the early '90s and the Denny's chain was facing a lot of discrimination and diversity lawsuits. I saw doing business with me, an African-American woman, as the answer to both of our challenges.

I called the Denny's corporate offices every Monday morning at 10:30 for 2½ years. The company never took me seriously. It was too distracted by its troubles and many management changes.

Finally a man named Jim Adamson took over the company. As part of his briefing, someone told him about this woman who called every Monday at 10:30 a.m. "Well, what does she want?" he asked. He was told about my company and he immediately saw the same huge opportunity I did. Denny's not only bought my syrup, it used my face in national advertising, helping the chain with its image problems and giving me the national exposure I was looking for.

My company's relationship with Denny's lasted almost 10 years. It was a great run, but now Michele Foods is really too big for that account. It's a national brand in 10,000 retail stores across the country. We have our own 45,000-square-foot manufacturing facility in Cincinnati for making syrups and coffee syrups, copacking, and bottling.

The big dream that was born when I first eyed my great-great-great-grandmother's recipe 25 years ago has certainly come true. I love the idea that her emancipation led to my financial freedom. I like to imagine her sitting on that porch in Mississippi, the recipe in her pocket, patting her leg, thinking that someday women will be independent enough to do something great.

Of course, it wasn't easy, and I made a lot of mistakes along the way. I probably spent $150,000 developing the syrup. It shouldn't have cost that much. That's why I've made it my legacy to teach others how to turn their family recipes into businesses. Each month I teach a class called "From Recipe to Retail and Beyond." People come in with their family recipes right off the stove. I teach them how to formulate for manufacturing, the cost factor, and the business side of things.

And I share my philosophy: Anything the mind can conceive can be made manifest through hard work, perseverance, and faith.

I also tell folks to think about the treasures that might be in their grandmother's recipe box. So many people are looking for the next big thing. If you are still for a moment, you might just find that it's been waiting for you within your family all along.

That's the gift my great-great-great-grandmother gave me and the gift I give my family. Two of my daughters work with me in the business. The syrup is still our family treat. I'm the grandmother now, and each Sunday you'll find me making homemade waffles with honey cream syrup for my grandbabies.

You can learn more about Michele's story and syrups at Michelefoods.com.

Tying on Success

Shep and Ian Murray,
founders of Vineyard Vines, a specialty tie company

We are two brothers who hated commuting into Manhattan and hated our corporate jobs. So we walked away and made our dream come true: creating a company that celebrates our beloved Martha's Vineyard. There was just one hitch. We had to do it by charging up tens of thousands of dollars on credit cards.

Ian: We grew up spending every summer on Martha's Vineyard. We're big boating guys. We love to sail and fish.

Shep: I love the whole "back to basics" nature of the Vineyard. It's all about getting back to nature, spending time on the water with friends and family, clambakes, skipping stones, or riding bikes on the beach.

Ian: We sure did daydream about that time when we were working our first jobs out of college. My brother and I were living at home with our parents in Connecticut and taking the train into Manhattan each day. I was working for a small PR firm and I hated the job. I hated the commute.

Shep: I was working at an advertising firm. I liked the work, but I hated the attitudes. One boss literally told me I needed to think inside the box. He didn't like the way I was trying to think of ways to sell an ad campaign to a client.

That made me reconsider my boss and the whole corporate experience. Did I really want to become that person? To be promoted to that? I realized I didn't want that life.

I walked into my boss's office and said, "I quit. This isn't the place for me. And by the way, my brother and I are going to make neckties."

My acting team leader told me, "You're making a big mistake. You'll never be able to do anything on your own."

I called Ian and told him what I had done.

Ian: I guess I wasn't too surprised because we had been joking around about quitting for a long time. I took Shep's cue, went into my own boss's office, and told him I quit too.

That night we had a couple of drinks in the train's bar car on the way home. We told our parents, and our mom started to cry. "How could you give up those good jobs?" she wanted to know. "This is why you went to college."

Shep: But we explained that we weren't afraid to take the risk. We were more afraid to look back with regret that we didn't go for our dream.

We were inspired by the idea of making ties, taking a boring product and making it fun. Kind of like Richard Branson did with Virgin Atlantic Airways or Howard Schultz did with Starbucks. Here were people who had taken a staple of everyday life—a seat on an airplane, a cup of coffee—and made it into something great and exciting.

We wanted to do that with a necktie.

Ian: When I got my PR job right out of college, I went and bought one suit. I wore it every day for the entire time I was there. I had a couple of shirts. Every day I would wear one of my ties or borrow one of Shep's or my dad's ties. Whenever there was something interesting on it, people would comment.

We realized that for a man, as long as you change your tie you can create a new look. So we went looking for any ties with a fishing rod or a golf club that wasn't too blatant. But we couldn't find any.

Shep: That's what inspired our idea: to give men ties to wear to work that could celebrate and reconnect them to the recreational lifestyles they truly enjoyed.

We also noticed that there was nothing a man or a woman could buy in a Martha's Vineyard souvenir shop that was a reminder of the island and the great time he or she had on vacation. So we decided to make ties that represent the finer things in life, the things people really love.

Ian: Of course, we had no experience in the clothing business, and we had no money to finance our new venture. We figured we could learn the business because we both have always been entrepreneurs. I have a band, and we sell CDs and things. And Shep had a car-detailing business while he was in college.

For this money challenge we did what money experts tell you you're not supposed to do. We charged it.

Before we quit our jobs, we signed up for every credit card we could get our hands on.

Shep: That's where Ian's attention to detail came in handy.

Ian: With credit card cash advances, we could write a check for $5,000, and it would be interest-free for 90 days. I would pay it off with a new credit card on day 88. It's something you're not supposed to do because you can end up in a bad situation. But we were completely aware of what we were doing. It seemed like a better option than taking on a partner early on to get some money. And we couldn't go to the bank because no one believed in what we were doing. We rang up about $40,000 in credit card debt.

Shep: But we also had early signs that we were on the right track. We made 800 ties off the bat and sold all of them in the first few weeks.

We had four prints that were specific to Martha's Vineyard, things that reflected water and the island. One of the Martha's Vineyard stores also had a store on Nantucket. It sold the bluefish design over there. We sold just as many on Nantucket that first summer as we did on the Vineyard. That's when we realized our idea was bigger than the Vineyard.

Ian: Not everybody caught onto our idea right away. A lot of stores told us, "Men don't wear ties anymore." This was 1998, the height of the dot-com boom. There was a lot of casual wear at the office.

Our answer was "Look at what you're selling. Look at who you're selling to and what they're wearing it for." Men were still buying ties to wear to weddings, cocktail parties, and graduation. Our ties became conversation pieces. We were convinced men would pick up our ties before they would pick up a brown tie with red stripes on it.

Shep: We thought we might be done in three months. But Vineyard Vines just keeps growing. We can now dress men, women, and children from head to toe in our products. We long ago paid off that credit card debt. In 2006 we did $37 million in business. Our products are available in 600 stores across the country.

The idea is that we have this brand. It's all about a lifestyle.

Ian: It has been an incredible 10-year ride. Now guys riding the train into corporate offices are wearing our ties sporting lobsters, jeeps, sharks, beach scenes, and turtles.

But during this time we've also lost both of our parents to cancer. They each lived long enough to see our success to know that they don't have to worry about us.

The sobering experience of losing both our parents has definitely kept us grounded. It's also given us a focus for our charitable giving. We tend to support cancer causes as well as organizations that reflect our love of the water.

Shep: To anyone who is thinking about leaving the corporate world behind and taking the leap, I would encourage you to go for it. At the very least, start doing something on the side and see how it goes.

Let that commuting time be your dream time. It's all about finding your passion and having no regrets when you look back. Is the risk as big as it feels? People tell us we're gutsy for walking away from our jobs, but we knew if Vineyard Vines didn't work out, we could always go back and get the same kind of jobs.

Ian: But it looks like there will be no more train commuting for us. No more days when the big decision is "Do I ride the train sitting forward or backward?"

Shep: That's true, but a lot of guys on those trains are now wearing Vineyard Vines ties.

You can learn more at vineyardvines.com.

Daryn's Takeaways

· ·

Shep and Ian bring to life the idea of doing what you love. It's not that making neckties was their calling. Rather they really loved the Martha's

Vineyard lifestyle. Claiming that love and passion led them to an incredibly lucrative business and a way to celebrate that lifestyle.

I believe people are drawn to authenticity and passion. If the brothers had dreamed up Vineyard Vines with the idea of making a zillion dollars, I don't think they would be experiencing the same level of success.

No matter how impractical, what is your passion? What do you enjoy in your time off? How could you turn that into vacation into your vocation?

Big, Beautiful, and Bodacious

Barb Wilkins and Lorna Ketler,
cousins and owners of Bodacious Lifestyles Incorporated

We're two curvy cousins. We are large in everything
we do and how we live our lives. We became frustrated that we couldn't
find the kind of fun, sexy fashion that we craved, so we stopped looking
around for clothes to fit us and created our own boutique and fashion
line. Together we are Bodacious.

Our moms are sisters and are both wee and petite. We grew up
playing together and borrowing from each other's closets.

We still love clothes and fashion now that we're grown up. We also
love our bodies just as they are. (Barb likes to use the word "plump." It
sounds sweet to her. She also likes "cushy, soft, large, and curvy." And if
you need to know specifically, Barb wears size 20 and Lorna wears size 16.)

We say celebrate your body, whatever size you are.

But we didn't find a lot to celebrate when we tried to shop here in our
hometown, Vancouver, British Columbia. We always want to wear what is
in fashion right now. We just want to wear it in our size.

We found shopping to be so frustrating and humiliating at times, to
go into stores that had absolutely nothing for us. We felt neglected and
left out. We would walk into a store and ask, "Do you have anything that
would fit me?"

The clerk would say no.

Barb would say, "Well, that's a shame because I would really like to spend money here, but I guess I will go spend it somewhere else."

But she was thinking, "Where? Where am I going to go?"

That's when our conversation started. We would ask ourselves things such as "If we could imagine the perfect store, what would it be? What would we sell there? What would it feel like when you stepped in the door? What would it smell like?"

So we decided to create our own store and call it Bodacious! We don't call it a "plus-size" store—we don't like that term. We carry sizes 10 to 24, but we don't like putting a label on it. We believe it's possible that one day there won't be terms like that. There will just be clothes that come in different sizes, and the size on the tag will be the size of the garment.

> We live by the idea "Don't wait!" Don't wait for someone else to create what you're looking for. Don't wait to go for your dream.

We sell fashion-forward clothing. Not all styles translate into larger sizes, but a lot of them do. We offer the same styling, the same look, but cut to fit women's curves.

There's a misconception that all larger size clothing needs to be so long that it covers your whole body and your bum. But that isn't the most flattering look. For example, we think shirts should be shorter than that, falling at the hipbone.

We also offer a completely different shopping experience. Ordinarily when you're curvy, shopping for clothes is a matter of finding something that fits, not of choosing one color or style over another. At Bodacious women feel welcome and celebrated. We have a great variety of styles to fit different body types.

Our boutique is 100 times better than we even imagined it could be, but it certainly wasn't easy getting started. The first challenge was financing and how to get it.

We went to a local credit union that's known around here for giving loans to women. Even with our good business plan, the bank manager didn't agree until we said, "Oh, our husbands both have jobs." Even with that they gave us only a $5,000 line of credit and a $5,000 loan. That's what we started our business on: $10,000.

We were able to start small, though, because we began as a consignment business. There was no inventory to buy—we just emptied our own closets. Soon we had other women eager to consign with us.

In the very beginning we discovered one designer and featured her. Then we added one rack of new designs. Those all did very well and we began to build on that.

By our third year of business, we looked at each other and said, "I hate dealing with consignment."

At that point about 30 to 40 percent of our sales was new designs. We decided to take the leap. We called all our customers and asked them to collect their items. The rest we donated to charity. The next day we had our best day ever in the store.

It turned out to be the right decision at the right time. It wasn't in our original plan, but it's where the business took us, and we've learned to listen to the business.

From that first $10,000 we expect to make a half million dollars this year and double that next year. Our own label and manufacturing are starting to take off. The Bodacious label now features a wrap-dress design in many colors, a kimono-style dress, and polka dot flip skirts with beautiful angel knit tops.

We're getting a lot of interest from other retailers who want to carry our line and we're looking at opening a second store.

The best part is that we get to wear the pretty and feminine fashions we were craving.

And we love changing the way women think and talk about their bodies. It's really about changing the thought that your body is not OK. Women seem to encourage other women to self-deprecate all the time. But we're not about that. We truly welcome women of all sizes here. If you're too small to wear our clothes, you can buy some of our accessories.

We live by the idea "Don't wait!" Don't wait until you're a certain size to buy yourself pretty clothes. Don't wait for someone else to create what you're looking for. And don't wait to go for your dream.

That very thing you're looking for might be a great idea for a business. Every day make sure you do something to move toward your goal. Get it out there. Tell people about it.

As for the money, you will be surprised how little money you can live on while your dream is getting started.

So go for it! Go live your big, bodacious life and dream!

You can find out more at bodacious.ca.

Daryn's Takeaways

· ·

I love how Barb and Lorna throw the dictionary out the window! They don't let someone else's definitions of beauty, fashion, and size define them or their customers. They deserve beautiful clothes because they say so! And if there was no store to support that idea, well, they would open one for themselves.

I wish I could put their infectious laughs in this book. They are laughing at the critics and laughing with the joy they create for themselves and their customers.

In what ways are you letting other people's beliefs or assumptions define you? What would you love to have that doesn't exist in your world? Is it something you could create for yourself and others?

Abundance on Aisle 6

Tessa Greenspan,
owner of Sappington International Farmers Market

My story is what can happen when you don't keep your
eye on your investments. But it's also a testament to how you can dig
yourself out of almost any hole. I run Sappington International Farmers
Market, one of the most successful independent markets in the country.
My experience sure didn't start out that way.

Investing in the market seemed to be such a good idea back in 1981.
My husband, Stanley, and I were raising our two children in St. Louis. We
both had a background in the produce business, and I thought investing in
this particular market would build a nest egg for our retirement.

My thinking wasn't totally off base. In my twenties, when my children
were very small, my husband and I had a little store. We sold flowers
and fruit. I noticed we were selling to a lot of people who had trucks and
would set up fruit stands on corners. When I saw the amount of money
they were making, I thought, "I can do that!"

I bought a big old red truck, which I had no idea how to drive, but
I found an empty parking lot and learned. Then I found an empty lot
across the river from St. Louis in Pontoon Beach, Illinois, and I was in
business. I went to market every morning, picked up a load, and set up
the corner fruit stand.

I made sure I looked the part, wearing overalls and a straw hat. Many of my customers thought I grew the produce myself. Not only was the business very lucrative, I learned a lot about fruit and produce. I learned fruit has a better-looking side, just like some people.

We sold that business in 1980, and my husband became a wholesaler. I settled into a life of helping him with his books, raising children, and doing a lot of charity work. That's when I came upon what I thought would be a fantastic investment opportunity, buying into what was then called Sappington Produce.

It was an old place that had been a grocery and fruit stand. I invested with partners I had known for 20 years, a family that owned a chain of grocery stores. I suggested we buy the old business and turn it into more of a fruit stand, adding cheeses and a few meats.

I put up a chunk of money. The other partners basically ran the business. Honestly I wasn't paying attention at all. I now take full responsibility for that. I figured I could just concentrate on my retirement activities and let my investment grow.

Unfortunately an unattended garden only grows a bunch of weeds. I was shocked in 1986 to discover that the business was hundreds of thousands of dollars in debt, and the other partners planned to declare bankruptcy! That was my wake-up call.

I took a look at the books for the first time in years and found that instead of the cushy nest egg I was planning on, I had $413,000 in debt. Furthermore if I, too, walked away, many businesses would be left empty-handed. That was simply unacceptable.

The first thing I did was take responsibility, not for blowing the money but for not paying attention. Trust me, that will never happen again in my life. Then I rolled up my sleeves and got to work, running a large business in which I had no experience, fixing a large problem unlike anything I had ever experienced.

I sent a letter to all of the vendors explaining the situation and promised that somehow, some way, all debts would be paid back in full if they would just be patient. This was going to be some challenge because the IRS also wanted $40,000 in back taxes.

Before I truly got to work I had to forgive my other partners. I realized that being angry with them for this mess was only going to take away energy from me to deal with the challenges I faced. So it was very important for me to forgive and let it go. That doesn't mean I forgot. It just meant I wasn't pulling my hair out and could concentrate fully on the store.

It then became a matter of putting one foot in front of the other. Each day I would go to the bank, and I would also take some time to listen to tapes on positive thinking in my car. I would give myself a little time to walk around the local park, pray, and collect my thoughts. I asked for the strength and guidance to get through this. That was vital because there were battles to fight each day.

Sometimes that meant playing the heavy. I discovered an employee who was giving a group of employees so-called employee discounts. She would ring up one item and give the employee the rest for free. She had to go, along with a number of other employees.

The first time I had to pay the remaining employees, I had to dip into my own savings. I took out a second mortgage on my home. I sold all my stocks—anything to stay in business. I didn't take a salary for five years. There I was in my early forties digging myself out of the deep, dark hole that was supposed to have been my nest egg.

It took me more than five years, but I did it! I finally paid off every cent of the $413,000! It was now time to make a big decision—close the store or sell it. Instead I chose to keep it open. That might not seem practical in this era of big discount grocery chains. I knew in order to make it as an independent store, I had to turn Sappington into a unique destination and quality shopping experience.

That is exactly what you find when you come to the market today. We are in a building twice the size of the original market. But when you walk in, you find an old-fashioned, farm-fresh, friendly place where it's a pleasure for families to shop together. The walls and ceiling are lined in wood. There's an elevated toy train that goes around the whole store.

I give tours to children, showing them how produce makes it from the farm to the store. I let them taste different products and give each one a coupon, inviting them to bring their parents and grandparents back. They always do.

We sell everything here, from groceries to 200 kinds of cheese, meats, organics and natural foods, soda, wines—everything a shopper could want, so shoppers don't have to go to two or three stores to get everything they need. In fact I changed the name to Sappington International Farmers Market because we sell foods from 16 different countries.

We've gone from owing to giving. There's a wishing well at the store, and every month we pick a different charity. The charity receives whatever money is in the wishing well, and I match up to $400. We've given away more than $50,000 during the past 10 years just from the wishing well.

I like to think that inspiration is the most valuable product that Sappington offers. I want people to know that when they make up their minds, they can do anything if they simply decide they can.

I'm actually thankful for all the challenges I've faced. I could not and would not have learned so much about running a successful business without all the adversity. But I'm not alone or special. We're all meant to do great things. We're all meant to have abundance. It's just a matter of deciding to tap into what's waiting for you, even if it takes hard work and determination to find it.

The so-called nest egg investment certainly turned out differently from what I had planned. In the end it is a thriving business and a fine financial asset. I just had no idea it would also be the investment tool that would teach me how I would live my life.

You can learn more about Tessa Greenspan and Sappington International Farmers Market at sappingtonfarmersmkt.com.

Daryn's Takeaways

· ·

Tessa's story is a great example of how forgiveness is a gift you give yourself. She chose to forgive the business partners that left her in a huge financial hole. She forgave because to keep being angry wouldn't serve her. It would simply eat up time and energy that she felt would be better spent on the job at hand: getting out of debt. Here's the energy budget idea at work again.

How can forgiveness serve you? What better use could you make of the energy you spend on anger?

Power Tools

Barbara K,
home fix-it diva, entrepreneur, and single mom

I created the largest woman-owned construction firm in New York City, only to watch my business and my marriage collapse in the wake of 9/11. Digging myself out of that personal, financial, and professional hole, I made my life my rebuilding project. Now I put tools in the hands of women to make them stronger in their own homes and lives.

If you've seen me on television, you know me as Barbara K. My mission is to empower women by showing them how they can fix and create things themselves in their own homes.

Just the thought that I have made my living as an entrepreneur in the construction business is surprising, given that there was nothing about my childhood that would have predicted this was the direction I would take. My father was an engineer, my mother a schoolteacher. There wasn't a self-employed bone in my gene pool. Yet somehow I was always thinking something up.

It started right after college. I was 20 years old and had no idea what I would do with my life. One day I heard my mother and her friends complaining about how hard it was to get things fixed or built around the house. One woman was angry that a contractor hadn't shown up. Another had lost a deposit. Still another was frustrated with her husband, who was always saying he would get projects done around the house but never did.

I decided I would be the one to get things done. I went to the local print shop and with $60 I had borrowed from my dad had some business cards printed. I established a list of services that women might need done in their homes: painting, carpentry, plumbing, gutter cleaning, general fix-it jobs.

Of course, I had no idea how to do these jobs myself. I figured I would take care of that part later. First I needed to line up work. I went down to the local shopping plaza every day from 9 to 5 and approached women as they came out of the grocery store, offering them my services.

Suddenly the phone started ringing at my parents' house where I was still living. "Barbara," my mother would say, "there's this lady on the phone who says she needs her house painted. What are you up to?"

At that point I was figuring out how to get the work done. I thumbed my way through the local *Penny Saver*, taking down names and numbers of local painters, carpenters, and plumbers.

Once I had checked out their references and work, I would pick up the tradespeople in my dad's 1976 Buick Le Sabre and deliver them to the job.

One time a carpenter said to me, "You should really know how to do this work if you're selling it." He gave me his tool belt. I just remember how heavy it was and how it weighed me down. I couldn't know at the time that I was doing the first bit of research for the biggest part of my future business.

First, though, there was a lot more growth and then a big crash.

I had a large number of women calling me for a variety of jobs when I decided to take the next step. I wrote a letter to the local IBM corporate offices and told them I had established a small crew of workers, electricians, and carpenters. I was here if there was any work that IBM needed.

When nothing came from that letter, I called the man in charge 25 times. He finally told me to come up to the office, where he agreed to give me a two-year deal to do IBM's small contract work.

From there I started acquiring some big projects as I grew my business into a successful construction company. We were doing $40 million in business, including some of the largest corporate build-out projects in New York City. I was barely 30 years old. I also managed to get married and have a baby somewhere in all this business building. But the good times didn't last.

By the summer of 2001, it was clear my marriage was in trouble. By the early days of September, my husband and I knew it was over. My husband was moving to South Beach with another woman. It was just my young son, my booming business, and I. Four days later 9/11 happened. My business came crashing down with those World Trade Center towers.

Most of my business at that point was in the financial district and midtown Manhattan. In fact just the day before, I was in the NASDAQ office on Liberty Street measuring for a new project. But after 9/11 everything stopped in the world of corporate construction. In this business you need to keep cash flow coming in or it's over. In my case, it was over.

Not only that, but I was in a ton of debt. I was scrambling to pay mortgages and was getting sued. Anything that could go wrong did go wrong. However, even in the depths of my despair I was learning some important lessons.

First, I realized if I could somehow find the will to get out of bed in the morning, I could also take the time to acknowledge what was important. It might sound like a cliché, but I could see that I had my son and my health.

I asked myself what was special about me. Everyone has something. I took stock of what I was good at and and what I wasn't at that point in my life. (I've since learned that this is something I need to do periodically.)

And I realized that at heart I'm a serial entrepreneur. I can add water to anything and make it grow. I took the home repair business and built it into a successful and recognized commercial construction company in New York City. I could do something like that again. After all, I had been named one of Crain's 100 Most Influential Women in Business in 2000.

Then pieces of inspiration began to appear. The first piece came the holiday season of 2001. My 4-year-old received a basketball net as a present and he wanted me to hang it up. I realized I didn't have a hammer. My ex-husband had taken the toolbox!

Of course he had the toolbox, for even when I was this powerful woman with my own construction business, I wasn't empowered inside my home. I was a damsel in distress, always turning to my husband to do odd jobs around the house. It occurred to me that other women were probably in the same situation or even worse.

That's when I identified my new mission: I could help women feel empowered in their own homes. As women, we know how to make a cake, clean, and—thanks to Martha Stewart—crochet the perfect doily, but we can't do basic fix-it jobs around the house. I set out to change that.

> I realized that at heart I'm an entrepreneur. I can add water to anything and make it grow.

The first step was to create a brand that marketed a line of tools and guidebooks for the home to women in the area of home improvement, where they lacked confidence. Barbara K tools are designed ergonomically to fit a woman's hand and aesthetically to suit her mindset. For instance, the hammer is curved with rubber on the grip. It's nonslip, cushioned, and slightly lighter, making it more comfortable to hold.

I also incorporated a fashion element. No novelty pink tools here. I decided to make all Barbara K tools gray and blue. The gray symbolizes strength and security. The blue is the style touch that makes a utilitarian product fashionable.

I was all set with my great idea, but I had no capital. I looked online to learn how to write a business plan and I raised enough money to have a prototype of the tool kit box made.

In 2004 Barbara K products were in just about every major retailer across America. Bloomingdale's, JCPenney, Linens 'n Things, Macy's. They were all on board. By 2005 so were Target, Avon, Ace Hardware, and select Home Depot stores.

There was just one problem. My great idea, my fabulous tools sold, but they weren't a breakout success because no one knew who Barbara K was. I was failing. By the time 2005 came along, many retailers didn't reorder.

Here I was having to scramble again, only this time I had investors breathing down my neck and 29 people depending on me for their jobs. Talk about pressure.

I know now that I was too aggressive in getting my products distributed, too aggressive in our product development and infrastructure costs without having the history of this new category at retail. It was just too expensive to produce and market them and still make money. I learned I had to pull back.

That's exactly what I've done during the last couple of years. With TV appearances, a newspaper column, three books, and my role as AOL's exclusive home improvement coach, I'm becoming more and more widely known. I'm not just some woman on TV swinging hammers. I'm the woman who created tools to empower other women.

I know there are plenty of women out there who feel powerless either in their own homes or in their personal lives. To each one I say the same thing: Get out of bed each day and take hold of something that makes you feel powerful. Make small goals that will lead to accomplishments and then to bigger goals. My entire journey started with a stack of business cards and no know-how. Finding what you're passionate about will fill in the blanks and lead you in the right direction to fulfilling your dream.

You can find out more about Barbara K's empowering tools at barbarak.com.

Closing Thoughts

I hope you've enjoyed meeting these amazing, inspiring people. I feel as if I've won the media lottery in that it's my job to interview these kinds of folks every day. As we come to a close, I've put together a small scrapbook of some of the inspiring images I hope you will take with you as you go for your dreams.

What a wonderful feeling it is to watch Scott Rigsby cross the finish line at the Ironman Triathlon in Hawaii. Scott inspires me by showing how making tough choices can bring you rewards beyond your wildest dreams (page 28).

How can I not smile when I think about Sebri Omer and his hospital in Africa? This Ethiopian immigrant lives the American dream, then uses his good fortune to build a medical center in Ethiopia. "You don't have to wait to be a billionaire to help others," he told me. His example illustrates how true that is ((page 119).

An afternoon with Bill Montgomery will cure what ails you. Never have I met a man with a better outlook on life. Who would have thought a blind man could teach me to see? At 91 years old, Bill sees with his fingers and his heart as he creates his magnificent sculptures (page 34).

Leigh Hurst (far right) is the dynamo breast cancer survivor with a message, a sense of humor, and a passion for saving the lives of young women. She exemplifies the importance of listening to your gut, whether it's telling you your doctor is missing a diagnosis or urging you to spread the word about an important health issue. Ladies, Feel Your Boobies! (page 53).

I'm so glad to have photos of Kent Couch. How else do you appreciate what it means to strap a lawn chair to a bunch of helium balloons? Maybe you don't want to try this at home, but do take a cue from Kent, who refused to let go of a childhood dream (page 97).

Sweet Henri Landwirth brought a tear to my eye and a lesson to my heart. This amazing Holocaust survivor shows me the incredible things that can be created when you let go of hate and focus on love (page 123).

Marie Hesser and the ladies of The Elite Repeat shop show me the importance of what they call a "belief plan." They believed they could create the consignment shop of their dreams, and $1 million in sales later, they certainly have done that (page 132).

As Jill Youse stands surrounded by boxes of breast milk ready to be shipped to Africa, she reminds me that inspiration to improve the world can come from strange places. It also helps to have a slightly twisted sense of humor. Jill is funny and smart enough to try an idea that most people thought was crazy. I know there are a lot of orphans in Africa and empowered moms in the U.S. who are glad that she did (page 145).

And speaking of Africa, that's where you'll find former investment banker Alicia Polak as she builds the Khaya Cookie company. The women shown here were some of the first to join Alicia, who started the bakery to empower women in one of the poorest townships in South Africa. Alicia was willing to walk away from a job with a fat paycheck in order to find work that filled her heart. Her journey shows me that inspiration comes in steps and pieces, not all at once (page 169).

I hope that experiencing these wonderful stories helps each of you expand the idea of what's possible in your own life.

If you're looking for more, you'll find a new inspiring story each day at DarynKagan.com. If you have or know of a story that fits the theme "Show The World What's Possible!" please stop by the website and click on the box that says "Tell Me Your Story." There's a good chance I'll feature it on the website or in the next *What's Possible!* book.

Here's sending you the power to dare to dream you can make a difference.

—Daryn

Gratitude

· ·

The word "acknowledgements" doesn't cover the depth of what I feel toward the many people who have supported me and contributed to this book.

Most important, thank you to everyone I feature in these pages for taking your valuable time to share your stories and for allowing your journeys and lessons to come through me to touch countless readers.

Bill Beausay, it starts with your phone call saying, "You should write a book." Thanks for not listening to me when I told you, "I don't have time" and for providing the structure to make this project possible.

Lisa Berkowitz, you are my literary fairy godmother.

Uwe Stender, your dedication as a book agent is surpassed only by your soccer coaching skills.

Vicki Ingham, The Editor That Could. You polish, push, and make "Hooray" like no one. Without you, there is no book.

Doug Samuelson, where I see words, you see layout and design. Thank you for the beauty of this book, beyond what I could envision.

Paul Schur, you're the best brand builder ever to come out of Horace Mann Elementary School.

My late father, Stu, thanks for teaching each of us kids to get up and walk it off after we fall.

Mom...for always expecting the best.

My Sissy and Markagan for being my biggest fans.

Tripod for sitting on my lap through all the writing.

Darla Louise for looking up at me with those brown eyes telling me it was time to step away and go for a walk.